The State of Love from the Above!

Love Ecology for Self Psychology

Don't Be Love-Negligent; Be Love-Intelligent!

Rimaletta Ray, Ph.D.

Copyright © 2019 by Dr. Rimaletta Ray.

ISBN   Softcover   978-1-951469-17-7

All rights reserved. No part of this book may be reproduced or transmitted in any form or by any means, electronic or mechanical, including photocopying, recording, or by any information storage and retrieval system without express written permission from the author, except in the case of brief quotations embodied in critical reviews and certain other non-commercial uses permitted by copyright law.

Printed in the United States of America.

To order additional copies of this book, contact:
Bookwhip
1-855-339-3589
https://www.bookwhip.com

Epigraph

Life is a choice

Of having the right voice!

        The right frequency of it

           Determines its creation speed!

You either live with love acceleration,

Or get stuck with love frustration!

        Only shaking off the fun gaming stuff

      Can you develop a beautiful human life!

Birds will be singing in it,

And flowers around will fit;

        You'll become wise

      And build up your own love paradise!

So, make love construction mood

 Your everyday emotional food

        And let your thought elation

      Provide you with Love Inspiration!

Let's Focus on Love Education without Any Frustration!

Long Live the Belief in Love Without IF!

The Anatomy of Love Knowledge is in the Universal Storage!

(The Tibetan Proverb)
"If You Don't Want to Be Wise, Suffer!"

Book Incentive

The DNA of Love is designed From the Above!

Being spiritually dead or alive are the two opposites of Death and Life!

Our Spiritual Maturation is in Love Elation!

1. Love-Refining is in Self-Redefining!

Love Perfection is in Self-Resurrection!

Love is just a Word
until Someone comes and fills it up with Meaning!

(Self-Induction for Love Production)

I Can Roam Any Terrain with Love in My Vein!

2. Love Sincerity is the Universal Dexterity!

To begin with, "*Why is this book?*" There are zillions of books written about love, and my mission here is not to write another one. That's not my goal. Still more so because it's impossible *to outshine the Universal Love* that is instilled in us from birth and that is programmed in us with every sacred book. I am not going to criticize or to moralize with this book, either. My intention is *to love-inspire and hate re-wire,* re-connecting us all to the **LOVE SINCERITY OF THE DIVINITY** that we are not supposed to break with under any circumstances and in any life reality. *The technological invention is not an exception!*

Don't take love for granted; it is God granted !

We are all *pirates in the Ocean of Life,* if love is concerned. We start life with exciting expectations to find a rich treasure, to invest it into our creative plans, to attain the state of giving, but we finally depart from this life with a lot of regrets. All the pirates have always had a specially designed **CODE OF BEHAVIOR** at the sea of life, and they had to stick to it religiously. *This book is the Code of Love as I see it.* It can always be enriched or modified by you.

Experience is the best teacher for the teachable!

We have become too neurotic, chaotic, hysterical, troubled, and too electronically overpowered. *The Codes of Love* that I present in this book for your quick X-raying are very simple. *Every code is squeezed into a page-long information* that can be interpreted in a personal way. They all rhyme because a poetic word goes better inward. These codes are my modest attempt to re-direct some lost souls from the dark side of life to the light one of love and loving.

Will your life more! That's the Love Law!

We are part of the **REALITY OF LOVE** that has a twisted shape now, and it worries me because we started forgetting the key rule of life:

Be Loving No Matter What; Love is Your Full Time Job!

3. Don't Be Crowd-Bewitched! Give Love the Freedom of Speech!

(An Inspirational Booster)

When we over-rationalize love,

We get cut off from the Love Above

    True love is leaving our guts,

      And it's becoming uguts! (Italian slang for nonsense)

In the tech era of digital connection,

  We get caught in a disconnection

      Of our face-to-face inspection

      And a soul-to-soul reflection!

We lose love mentally and emotionally

  Because we expose ourselves only digitally!

      Our heart-to-hearts and tete-a-tetes

      Happen in hasty superficial fits!

We read the text messages once or twice,

But we don't see the partner's eyes!

      Nor do we sigh or romanticize

      His or her heart's size!

We are expecting a soul mate,

But we continue to rate

Every one's love track

By the size of his / her money sack!

    Nor do we want to commit

    To a long-term mutual fit!

We break up, make up, or set up,

Without thinking twice "What's up?"

    We fall in love with the virtual reality,

    Often devoid of human sanity!

Hence, love goes in reverse

Of its natural human course!

    Men get attracted to handsome males;

    Women prefer frailness to real maleness!

Is it another case of Sodom and Gomorra,

Or should we see it as the saddest "umora"? (Sad laugh in Russian)

    True, the choices we make, dictate the life we live,

    But the Nature's choice is sacred still!

And we are not heading to a destruction

Of our life-long human function!

    We are just learning to respect love

    In the mind and the heart's personal gulf!

We need to stop our love over-rationalization

And accept or give love without frustration!

Love without a sex role transmission

May well be a God-given mission!

But if the choice is made in a personal net,

It's not a free country' business to mess the outlet!

Love is in the eye of the beholder,

Not in the mass media's molder!

So, let's practice what we preach

And give love the Freedom of Speech!

Be nice and loving and beware

To protect your love's eyes and ears everywhere!

May Love in You

Preside for the Two!

4. Let's Change the Immediate Gratification Reality of Self-Vanity!

The State of Love in the society, backed up by an exponential growth of technology is going through the **Revolution of Self-Consciousness.** Different sex emancipation movements are the manifestation of love liberation.

But we are not getting better, we are becoming bitter!

I am not a prude, but I am not an indifferent educator, either. When the idea to write this book struck me, I had a lot of arguments against a new venture in my fifteen inspiring books adventure.

<u>*We are living at the time when physical attraction is in action while soul connection is in retention!*</u>

Young people can hardly manage their sex drive because they suffer from a lot of love frustration due to the lack in **LOVE EDUCATION**. They surrender to the demands of their sexual expression without any love obsession. Masturbation has become a sex relief invasion.

Pornography is substituting love sanctity and personal gravity!

Girls' sex-revealing way of getting dressed puts us in dismay. Even middle school kids entice an opposite sex with a fun-looking, mindless fest. Mind enrichment and soul refining are not in self-designing!

Sex-obsession is in session!

I am painfully conscious that we need to re-direct our attention from sex tension to a new, time-dictated self-reflection that'll result into a much healthier society with *a digitized enrichment of the notion of love*.

Science is gradually obliterating the creative function of men in procreation. The sperm banks and the services of sperm donors are getting more and more popular. Other than that, women get lazy with having a natural birth delivery. Many gay love-devoted men feel naturally entitled to raise their own kids which they can also do excellently and the society should not stand in the way..

Cheating has become a real curse and a personality ruining force!

But love is encoded in our DNA, and our evolutionary role is to reverse the wrong course. Religion has generated the spiritual growth of a man, but it is pressing the human nature too much with the concept of a sin that can hardly be processed by a contemporary, technologically enhanced mind of the young.

Spiritual maturation of a soul is our common goal!

We obviously need to learn to trace our love failures back to the cause and inhabit our souls with other good or better self-growth. Happiness is based on love, and it cannot be sudden. It must be gradually distributed by the spirit that connects the mind and the heart for the whole life.

"The Universe is structured so that every person can be born to be a Christ, a Buddha, or a Zarathustra, but we need to teach a human being to obtain the wings to fly.

Life is the Rhythm of the Music of Love that we need to perceive!"

(Nikola Tesla)

Let's Redirect Love-Frustration to Love Regeneration!

5. Nothing is Impossible if We Make Our Inner Change Irreversible!

(See the Holistic Paradigm of Self-Resurrection below)

Self-Evolution is in breaking through Love Pollution!

Love Shouldn't be dying from the Corruption and Lying!

You Can Roam any Terrain with Love in Your Vein!

6. My Love Grows with You!

(An Inspirational Booster)

With your love in me,
I am full of spiritual glee!

    With you, I magnetize
    With my mind and the eyes!

With you, I don't ever whine,
I shine!

    Everything I do,
    Is in unity with you!

Love is my act of sharing, giving, and forgiving;
<u>*Love is My Being!*</u>

"Love creates a new circuitry of energy in the body. It is our prana tube". (Sadh guru)

Create the Space of Love
Inside, Below, and Above!

Look into the Mirror of Your Soul and Be overly Whole!

(The Antenna of Love is connecting us to the Above)

Your Soul is Charged by the Love's Surcharge!

Table of Content

Book Incentive - *The DNA of Love is Designed from the Above!* ---pp. 5-14

1. Love Refining is in Self- Redefining!

2. Love Sincerity is the Universal Dexterity!

3. Don't Be Crowd-Bewitched! Give Love the Freedom of Speech!

4. Let's Change the Immediate Gratification Reality of Self-Vanity!

5. Nothing is Impossible if You Make Your Inner Change Irreversible!

6. My Love Grows with You! (An Inspirational Booster)

For the Reader to First Consider - *Love Growth is Multi-Dimensional!* --pp. 23-28

1. Life is Exceptional if it Becomes Multi-Dimensional!

2. Those Who Defy the Gravity of the Common - Fly!

3. Love Must Be Self-Programmed!

4. Self-Induction is the Basis for Love Production!

5. Love Equation needs the Auto-Suggestive Invasion

Introduction to Love Induction - *Don't Take Love for Granted; It Is God Granted!* ---pp. 30-39

1. The State of Love is the Unity with the Above! (An Inspirational Booster)

2. The Art of Loving is at the Universal State of Living!

3. We Create Our Own Golden Age Now; WOW!

4. View Love with a New Look Every Day and Work for it Today!

5. Love - Resurrection is in Love Reflection!

6. Holistic Self-Creation is in Love Elation!

7. Activate the Divine Code of Your DNA. Do Not Love Sway!

8. A New Renaissance of Thought and Action is in Function!

9. Our Transformation is in Love Elation!

Part One – *Computer-Coding Demands Love Re-Molding!* ---pp. 41-55

1. "The Whole of Love lies in the Verb Loving!"

2. Don't Love Automatically or Statically! (An 0Inspirational Booster)

3. Love Elation is in Self-Revelation!

4. *Digital Transformation is in Self-Reformation!*

5. *Souls Grow Stale from Love Routine; Don't Let it Spin!*

6. <u>*Love Resurrection is in Love Intelligence Perfection!*</u>

7. *To Reach a New Love Site, Scan It with Your Inner Might!*

8. *Place Your Love Realms on the New Awareness Stems!*

9. *Love Oasis Grows First on the Social Basis!*

10. *Soul-Refining is in Self-Redefining!*

11. *Place Your Love Realms on New Awareness Stems!*

12. *Evolution vs. Stagnation is at the Core of the technological Elation!*

13. *The Channels of Your Perception are cleared by an Aware Reception!*

14. *Self-Enlightenment (An Inspirational Booster)*

Part Two – *Love Fractals* **/** *The Know -How of Living in five dimensions of Being* --**pp. 57-68**

1. *Don't Let Your Love Just Happen!*

2. <u>*Love Fractals are the Life Functional Matters!*</u>

3. *Love Gravity is Formed. by the Fractals of Self-Symmetry*

4. *Love Creation is in Inner Illumination!*

5. *We are One in Love, and Love is One in Us!*

6. *Deep Love Discontent wakes up a Personal Intent!*

7. *New Stuff is in the Code of Love!*

8. *The Job of Love is the Eternal Stuff!*

9. *To Connect to a New Love's WI-FI, Follow the Route of What, Where, and Why.*

10. *We Need to Live in Line with the Space -Time Twine!*

11. *The Anatomy of Love Knowledge is in the Universal Storage!*

Part Three – *Love Zones* **/** *Book Structure – Five Main Zones of Love* --**pp. 70-76**

1. *The Growth of Love from the Above.*

2. *Love Myth is a Multi-Dimensional Bliss!*

3. *Shape Your Love's Mold by a Personally Despised Love Code!*

4. **<u>*The Auto-Suggestive Love Coding for Self-Molding!*</u>**

5. *Carpe Diem! Seize the Day!*

To Master Love's Devine Stuff, Learn to Love!

(The Main Love Zones of the Book to form the Mind's Nook)

Love Zone One – *The Love Risk Zone* **/** Exaltation and Love Elation –

Physical Dimension --- **pp. 78-105**

1. To Have Love, Be Love!

2. Love is always an Equation! (An Inspirational Booster)

3. Love is a Partnership with God!

4. Love's Security is in Our Spiritual Maturity.

5. Love Intelligence without Negligence

6. Love on Earth must be a Mentally Conquerable Force!

7. The Unconquerable Libido

8. Sexual Re-Lay is at Play!

9. <u>Love is a Freedom of Choice and Your Personal Voice!</u>

10. Love Grows with You! (An Inspirational Booster)

11. The DNA of Love is Encoded in the Brain's Stuff!

12. Simplify Your Life with Being Alive! (An Inspirational Booster)

13. Re-Invent Yourself in Every Cell!

14. Be a Self-Guru; Love is a Seasonal Phenomenon, too!

15. Let's Regain the Sense of Shame!

16. **<u>Moral De-Magnetization is now in Elation!</u>**

17. Hasty Loving Ends in Whining!

18. The Gift of Love Must be Instilled by the Returned Love

19. Love Magnetism is Charged with Self-Reformism!

20. Love is Never Confusing; It's Soul Musing!

21. <u>The Inner Dignity of the Whole forms the Aristocratism of the Soul!</u>

Love Zone Two - *Breach of Trust Zone* **/** Expectation and

Justification (Emotional Dimension)-- **pp. 107-141**

1. Illusion vs. Delusion

2. <u>Any Soul's Recovery is in Love Discovery!</u>

3. The Harmony of Love is a Very Fragile Stuff!

4. Love or Lust; Who Can I trust?

5. *Love Pollution has become Our Common Social Constitution!*

6. *Moral Intelligence and Love Magnetism without Racism and Sexism.*

7. *Love Intelligence is Hard to Obtain and Regain!*

8. *The Authentic Love from the Above is becoming Viral Now. WOW!*

9. ***Piracy in Love kills the Love Stuff!***

10. *If You are Love-Lenient, Self-Demagnetization becomes Expedient!*

11. *Sex without Love is a Bluff! (An Inspirational Booster)*

12. *Do Love Induction for a Better Love Function!*

13. *Put the Strain on Your Subconscious Brain! (An Inspirational Booster)*

14. *Motivate Your Love with Discipline and Consistency Stuff!*

15. *The Next Step in Love Defining is living Without Lying!*

16. *A Family Life's Refining is in a Man's Role Redefining!*

17. *What Women Want for their Love Reward.*

18. *Emotional control is our Love Gravitational Goal!*

19. *The Method of Substitution in Love - Hate Infusion*

20. *Active Meditation on the Love Beach of the Self-Reflection Switch!*

21. *The Unity of the Hearts and Minds Binds!*

22. *Don't Let the Dirty Sex Drive Ruin Your Love Life!*

23. *To Soul- Rewind, Be Kind to the Unkind!*

24. *Put on the Crown of the king / Queen and Be Serene!*

Love Zone Three — *Self-Love Zone* **/** Love Awareness

Mental Dimension-- pp. 144 -172

1. *Love Stuff Begins with Self-Love!*

3. *Love Intelligence without Negligence.*

3. *Love is a Rainbow of Enlightened Consciousness!*

4. *Love Realism without Skepticism*

5. *The Authenticity of Self is in the Spiritualized Love Cell!*

6. *Not to Love Drain, Have the Love Police in the Brain!*

7. *To Be Highly Love-Rated, Become Love-Acculturated!*

8. *The Love Gravity Connection is Grounded in Self-Reflection!*

9. *Self-Patronage in Love*

10. *Being Content with the One that God put on Your Path is a Must!*

11. *The Stream of Consciousness Technique is the Love Peak!*

12. *You Radiate What You Emanate!*

13. <u>*Love Sanity is in Self-Gravity!*</u>

14. *Committment is Me; Commitment is my Philosophy!*

15. *The Hypnosis of Social Conditioning (An Inspirational Booster)*

16. <u>*Self-Sufficiency Attracts More than Sexuality!*</u>

17. *Keep the Speaking Form in a Dignified Uniform!*

18. *Take Care of the Gene of Your Love's Hygiene!*

19. <u>*Conquer the Mouth with Your Love Wows!*</u>

20. *Only the Independence of the Spirit will Love Inspirit!*

Love Zone Four – *Self-Sufficiency Zone* **–** Faith and Inner Grace

Spiritual Dimension-- **pp.173-193**

1. *Your Love Wings are in the God's Ins.*

2. *To Deserve Your Very Best, Be on the Spiritual Quest!*

3. *Spiritual Maturity Guarantees your Love's Security!*

4. *Self-Salvation is in Love Maturation!*

5. *Remove Your Love Warts and Stop Living Backwards!*

6. *The Mind + Heart Link is in Sync with the Universal Wink!*

7. *Sincerity is the Soul's Dexterity!*

8. *Life and Death as One are ruled by the Tongue!*

9. *The Ability to Love fills Your Inner Space with Grace.*

10. *Inner Dissonance must Give Way to Love Consonance!*

11. <u>*The Soul's Health is Our Wealth!*</u>

12. *Release the Mind + Heart Peace!*

13. *The "Monkey Mind" is Never Kind.*

14. *Forgive, Forget, and Let Go; Be Fast, Not Slow!*

15. *Don't Let Anger and Hate Infiltrate Your Fate!*

16. *Halfway in Love is a Bluff!*

17. *The Art of Aging is Love Engaging!*

God in His Digital Form is Becoming Our New Universal Uniform!

Love Zone Five- *Love Zone Five-* Oneness with Love from the Above

Universal Dimension)--- **pp. 195-205**

1. The Sense of Measure is the Universal Treasure!
2. Exceptionality in Love is the Universal Stuff!
3. Use Autohypnosis for Self-Prognosis!
4. Observe the Diet of Your Love's Surf!
5. Don't Bluff the Purity of Love!
6. True Love is Not a Myth; It's a Bliss!
7. The Law of Attraction is in Love Function!
8. The Right and the Left Brains in Sync Love Click.
9. Don't Love Switch; Practice What You Preach!

Conclusion of Love Infusion!---------------------------------- pp. 207-214

1. Let's Spread Love Magnetism without Any "Ism!"
2. You Better Be Alone than with Whoever!
3. The State of love is the School from the Above!
4. To Be Highly Love Rated, Become More Love–Acculturated!
5. Self-Affirming is Self-Reforming!
6. The Art of Love is a Divine Stuff!
7. Let's Create the State of Love! (An Inspirational Booster)
8. **Love Intelligence is Our Life -Reverence!**

Learn the Art of Love from the Above!

Make Your Heart Smart and the Mind Kind; Be One of a Kind!

Self-Evolution Comes in Layers:

(Pictures by Galina Morrel)

Physical, Emotional, Mental, Spiritual, and Universal!

For the Reader to First Consider

Love-Growth is Multi-Dimensional!

The reality distortion field is filled with love defeat!

"There is no right person for anyone on the planet. Focus on becoming the right person for the man / woman of your choice yourself."
(Sadhguru)

Love is the Core of Every Life's Domain; Love is in Your Vein!

1. Love is Exceptional if it Becomes Multi-Dimensional!

I have touched upon our evolutionary growth in time and space in my previous five books, comprising the pyramid of the **HOLISTIC SELF-RESURRECTION** though self-revelation and self-growth that is multi-dimensional. These books consequentially are:

The Holistic Self-Actualization Pyramid / Books, featuring these stages:

5. Universal level	Self-Salvation	" Beyond the Terrestrial!"
4. Spiritual level	Self-Realization	" Self-Taming!"
3. Mental level	Self-Installation	" Living Intelligence or the Art of Becoming!"
2. Emotional level	Self-Monitoring	" Soul-Refining!'
1. Physical level	Self-Awareness	" I Am Free to Be the Best of Me!"

Loving is at the root of spiritual maturation, and <u>*love is multi-dimensional,*</u> too. The holistic paradigm of Self-Resurrection, presented above is a simple blueprint of the steps, meant to help you harmonize your inner self though new knowledge and inspire yourself with new abilities, the most vital of which is **THE ABILITY TO LOVE** and *generate love in return.* We realize now that a regular way of the commonly programmed life – *falling in love, making a career, getting married, raising children, see them succeed in their life, and getting peacefully old* is not a complete scenario of life.

Raising self-consciousness and realizing a unique personal mission of life are our priorities that can be accomplished only against the background of love for oneself, for the home country, the loved ones, the kids that we bring into this world, the work that helps us in self-realization, the world that we are getting united with at the click of a finger now, and the Universal Field of Intelligence that we all perceive as God. A new positive slogan gets glued to the minds of many for whom *the* **AUTHENTICITY OF SELF** is to live without the society's evil spell! Spiritual maturity helps people declare,

I've Made a New Turn. I Love and I'm Loved in Return!

2. Those who Defy the Gravity of the Common - Fly; Those who Crawl - Die!

Dr. Frederick Bell, the author of a very scientifically enriching book *"Death of Ignorance"* writes that our basic soul light is both positive and negative, as everything else in the magnetically charged world. He applies the terms fire and water to **the masculine and feminine principles**, respectfully. Dr. Bell writes, *"As evolution advances, feminine souls display more of the fiery masculine qualities, while masculine souls take on the ethereal beauty of the feminine."*

Overcome the evil direction and become more civil in reflection!

Put in this light, our growing physical intelligence makes us understand that *it is pointless to verge a fight against gay movement.* Gay people are prone to their self-development as anyone else, and their choice is the matter of their own soul light and their own soul evolution. *The sincerity of love from the Above* is not the mass media's stuff!

<u>**Love and let love; it's a personal stuff!**</u>

The most important thing is the richness of a person's aware intelligence and the level of his / her growing self-consciousness! *Let's deprogram our brains without vanity, from religiousness to true spirituality!* Only a truly spiritual person can put his interests above his own because he / she is sure that one day the loved one will do the same in return. <u>**Meeting a person half-way is the love's way!**</u>

Love that starts at the highest *spiritual level* develops further at the *mental* one. If the intelligences of the two people click, they feel magnetized even more. They gradually develop a strong *emotional attraction* that finally resonates into the *symphony of the physically - uplifting love.* Such love energizes and spiritualizes, not depletes of the energy fits! This is what this book is about.

Make Love Ecology Your Personal Psychology!

3. Love Must Be Self-Programmed and Inductive, not Game Productive!

<u>Love Ecology is in the Auto-Suggestive Psychology!</u>

(For More, see the books on the Auto-Suggestive Psychology of Self-Ecology!)

(Auto-Induction for Self-Production):
Love is Me;
Love is My Philosophy!

4. Self-Induction is the Basis for Love-Production!

I Create the Space of Love.
Inside, Below, and Above!

Swimming in the Love Sea
Is My New Philosophy!

Let's Make the State of Love from the Above Our New Life's Gulf!

5. Love Equation Needs the Auto-Suggestive Invasion!

On the ladder of the fractal formation and our *spiritual maturation*, *(See below)*, there is our growing ability to love not just ourselves, our loved ones, the parents, kids, and friends. Every of my five books on Self-Resurrection has the part that presents love as *the core of every life domain,* not only the emotional one. (*See the book "Self-Taming)*

The ability to love means filling your inner space with grace!

The circle of the spiral gets wider as we are moving up, bettering. ourselves, level by level and rejoicing at the idea of becoming worthier of life and more loving it in its every manifestation. *This is the process of a constant self-inductive and self-reflective character*. I remember a wonderful piece of advice the father gives to his daughter in the movie " *The Wedding Planner,*" showing her that love is a process.

"Appreciation grows into respect; respect grows into like; like grows into love"

Obviously, if love starts at the highest *spiritual leve*l of compassion, consideration, and mutually shared values, it develops further at the *mental one*. If the intelligences and mental interests click, the two people feel magnetized even more and develop a strong *emotional attraction* that resonates into the symphony of *the physically - uplifting love.* Such love inspires, connects, spiritualizes, and energizes!

The end justifies the means!

The spiritualized intelligence and the **INNER GRACE** that the two people accumulate on the spiritualized intelligence track will resonate with the **RAISED SELF-CONSCIOUSNESS**. It will constantly remind us of the ultimate Universal stage of life that should be anticipated with awareness, inner peace and tranquility.

Self-Salvation Has a Sold Love Foundation!

I Kiss Your Soul !

Imaged by Heritage Auctions, HA.com

(Mark Chagall)

Be Faithful to Your Soul.
Love is Your Goal!

Introduction to Love Induction

Don't Take Love for Granted; It is God Granted!

If You are More Love Aware, You'll Never Be in Despair!

1. The State of Love is the Unity with the Above.

(An Inspirational Booster)

We are One with the Universe,

We are One with the Sun;

    We are One with everything

      Under the Sun!

We are One with the Earth,

We are One with the Moon ;

    We are One with the sky, the clouds,

      And the vegetation boom!

We are One with the animals

And this refreshing breeze;

    We are One with the birds

      And the autumn striptease!

We are One with all people that strive to survive,

We are One with those who passed by!

    In our life philosophy, we should unite

      The continents, the countries, and the like!

We are all of One Blood

In the Universal Gut!

Unity is Our Spiritual Glee;
Unity is Our Love Philosophy!

2. The Art of Loving at the Universal State of Living!

Love in its Universal sense is in recess now, and on the ladder of our love evolution we need to acquire the *spiritualized intelligence* and *spiritual maturation* of the most essential aspects of our being in five life dimensions: *physical, emotional, mental, spiritual, and universal.* It means obtaining the ability to love in a much broader sense. Every book *on Self- Creation,* presented above, features the steps of self-growth under the magnetic power of love.

" Life is not a circle, it's a spiral!" (Dr. Bell)

The circles of the love spiral get wider as we are moving up, bettering ourselves, level by level, rejoicing at the idea of becoming worthier of life and more loving it in its every manifestation. This is what we need to instill in our kids and the young people, going to college.

Our young people still have very little love education, if at all.

We accumulate spiritualized intelligence and such **INNER GRACE** in the process of self-growth, raising **SELF-CONSCIOUSNESS** on the way thorough the fundamentally holistic education that need to widen the students' horizons of a personal growth and the ways of *Self-Installation* in life. Professional Intelligence is not the final goal! Conscious *holistic self-growth* will constantly remind us of the ultimate, Universal Stage of life that should be anticipated with awareness, inner peace, and the desire for full Self-Realization in life.

It is the stage from which love eternally grows. That's why when we are lucky enough to meet a good person that we qualify as a soul mate, the feeling of an amazing mutual connection generates the butterflies in the stomach and *the spirit gets equipped with the wings to fly*. Only love can uplift us to the universal level of life without any strife!

The Talent of Love is a Boundlessly Universal Stuff!

3. We Create Our Own Golden Age Now; WOW!!!

We all know about the sacred value of love, but we are not aware of it. Instead of being in *the Flow of the Source* of life, we are in the flow of the chaos of life. We are still the victims of the life situations that like a negative vortex suck us in, making us helpless, fearful, doubtful, and constantly programmed **OBJECTS OF LIFE**, not its creative **SUBJECTS**.

Be ready to declare to yourself and the world, *I am Free to be the Best of Me!* Free yourself from the chaos of the incoming information. Focus on the life in yourself, free of any limitations, imposed by the mass media and the society. To heal the body or emotions, we need to go beyond the body and its sensations. In mathematics, that is considered to be the science of God, there is the infinite number, known as *the Fibonacci number*, re-discovered by Johannes Kepler in 1608. This number is *a paramount spiritual ideal* of all structures, forms and proportions.

It is also known as the **GOLDEN RATIO**, a special number that links the past and the present, approximately equal to *1,618.* This number is called a magic and holy symbol of life, and it, in fact, symbolizes the **RENAISSANCE OF OUR SOULS**, or the enlightenment of love in them. The time of our re-birth has come, and the beauty of life in its infinite forms reflects *the Golden Ratio* in our new thinking, speaking, feeling, and acting. The wonders of life, generated by the technological revolution mesmerize, and our individual role is to be in sync with these beautiful changes in our inward re-formation, governed by the Golden Ratio, too.

Let the Inner Symphony of Love Orchestrate Your Life's Stuff!

4. View Love with a New Look Every Day and Work for it Today!

The Universal Stage is the stage from which true love always grows. That's why when we are in love, the feeling of an amazing mutual unity in the ***universal, spiritual, mental, emotional, and physical*** stem of our Being uplifts the spirit and equip us with the wings to fly over any troubles, distance, forceful separation, wars, and even death. The evolution of our **SELF-AWARENESS** helps in saving love from the world-wide contagious *Americanization of Consciousness* that, like cancer, has spread its metastasis all over the world. Love takes a wrong road and can hardly survive in the money-based and fun-seeking chase in life because it turns into an ***impulsive, immediate gratification whim*** and, consequently, it becomes impersonal.

I like the Japanese proverb that helps us retain the sacredness of love in the new sex battle stuff. *"A husband and wife must be like a hand and eyes. When a hand aches, eyes cry. When the eyes cry, the hands wipe the eyes."* ***We have lost the bliss of this sacred myth!*** But we are still inspired and motivated to become better for the loved one! We need to share with someone what we have accomplished, transforming ourselves at each level together on the way to ***Self-Salvation*** *physically, emotionally, mentally, spiritually, and universally.*

Don't bury your exceptionality in life's banality!

So, this book is about focusing your **AWARE ATTENTION** on establishing the unity of the **MIND** and the **HEART** in five dimensions of life. This unity is the center of our biological field, ***the Merkabah*** circle *(See the "Flower of Life" By D. Melchizedek)*, connected ***to the Universal Informational Field.*** Tune in to the sacred heartbeat: of *21- 21- 21* or *Love – Love - Love!*

To Obtain Life Consonance, Let's Get Rid of Our Love Dissonance!

5. Love-Resurrection is in Self-Reflection!

Time is changing our reality exponentially, and our consciousness is changing with it, **altering the configuration of our sub-conscious mind** that has recorded our past lives and the love habits that had been formed by us for centuries on end and that need to be revised..

Our Heaven from birth is on Earth, not under it, or up Forth!

Every human being on Earth has his / her own unique design of self-consciousness that is, in fact, a very subtle *electro-magnetic field* around each of us. This field is formed by our thoughts, words, feelings and actions, and it has its high or low vibrations that are based on the **AUTHENTICITY** and **SINCERITY** of our goals in life. The feeling of love for oneself, the Mother Nature, the parents, the loved ones, the friends, and "thy neighbor" constitute our *Field of Love from the Above* that helps us expand the scope of our souls.

The moment a person betrays his inner core and starts swimming against the current of his / her essential, God-granted **LOVE STREAM,** he / she loses the guidance of the Source of love from the Above. We must stay in the love stream, magnetizing it with *the unity of our hearts and minds* that form the **MERKABAH**, the electro-magnetic center of our being

Our Psycho-Culture is in the Self-Monitoring Structure!

In sum, it's everyone's sole goal to work on preserving *the electro-magnetic core of love* in oneself and charging it with love energy as we do it with our smart phones. Self-Resurrection in love elation has the **LOVE PARADIGM** of - *Praying* (talking to God), *Meditating* (listening to God), and *Acting* (following God) or

Synthesis -Analysis – Synthesis!

To Have Love from the Above, Revisit Your Heart + Mind Gulf!

6. Holistic Self-Creation is based on Love Elation!

The new times are the times of our **TRANCENDENCE** into a new mode of life - new thinking, speaking, feeling, and acting that are generated by the technological evolution and the exponential growth of the means of seeing life through a celestially digitized perception of a new spiritual reality that is also a **NEW LOVE REALITY.**

The power of God is in everyone's thought!

The ever quoted religious and spiritual maxima *"God is Love!"* and *"Marriages are made in Heaven!* are commonly repeated, but we are still in search of *the godly love* in a man /woman while the spiritual deterioration of the best of God's creation is appalling now.

The skill to love in mass must be instilled and developed in us!

So, the first thing that we need to look for in a person is a **GODLY SPARK OF LOVE** in his / her heart and the drops of kindness in the actions, not his /her sexual orientation. The spark of love needs to be fueled in every one of us becoming the torch of love, like Danco's heart. According to the ancient legend, Danco tore his heart out of his chest to lighten up the way for the people, walking in darkness.

Love in sync with the soul; Be spiritually Whole!

Luckily and irreversibly, a present-day man has started perceiving himself as an integral part of the whole of life, not as a separate, fearful, society indoctrinated, and dependable personage who plays his part in the performance of life in which every role is scripted. The most advanced, well-read, and forward-thinking people activate their *new genetic code* and stand up for the uniqueness of their transforming self. They are swimming against the current of the generally accepted trend of *a savagely expressed love.*

"As it is Above, so it is Below!"

7. Activate the Divine Code of Your DNA. Do Not Love Sway!

Love is *the Cosmic Law of Unity,* and its divine paradigm never changes. Our prime goal in life is to retain the vibrations of the *Universal Super-Consciousness,* emanating love as the Source of our existence. Meditation practices connect us to the Source, switching our attention to the **INVISIBLE FIELD OF NOTHING** and helping us experience pure consciousness of self-transformation.

The Universal Intelligence calls on us to change our vibrations, *enter the Flow of Love from the Above* and become One with this source of life. In other words, love is a gradual raising of self-consciousness to *the fourth dimension* of life – its **SPIRITUAL VOLUME!**

The humanity is, in fact, on the way of getting to *the fifth Universal dimension* of light that, actually, is the love dimension, *the Christ Consciousness era, or the Golden Age* that we need to generate now.

<u>*Living means to become a Soldier of Love from the Above!*</u>

Such living is a constant striving to be in the radiate light of inner enlightenment, intelligence, creativity, emotional balance, simplicity and inner grace. Nikola Tesla was known to be a man who could totally control his emotions, being a man from the Balkans, the area of the Earth that is known for its very passionate men.*"I have learnt to control my emotions of love not to distract me from my ideas and not to blur my imagination that is the basis of all my discoveries."* (Nikola Tesla). Apparently, *sex control is the matter of will-power and character.*

The central message of any sacred book is "**I AM LOVE,**" *I am light! Be Like me!"* You are light, too! You do not need to prove it to anyone. *Just be yourself*! Just live NOW, not in the past, not in the ephemeral future. Smile, laugh, give the gift of your presence to others, love and be loved in return.

To Be a Happy Bee, Just Be!

8. A New Renaissance of Thought and Action is in Function!

Don't Just God-Declare; Be More Self-Aware!

We are now in the early stages of the technological evolution that brings together the digital, physical, and biological systems. We live at the time that maximizes human abilities. An honest, transparent relationship bliss is getting transferred into a digital myth!

"To find love, knock on the sky and wait for a reply! "

(Zen saying)

Wow! I Live Now!

9. Our Transformation is in Love Elation!

(An Inspirational Booster)

My soul transformation
Is in love elation!

With my love basis,
I am fearless and ageless!

I am less,
Than I can profess,

But I am more,
Than I was before!

My transformation is slow,
But it is on the go,

Far beyond the vision
Of my every new year's provision!

I am moving onward, upward, Godward!

<u>What is your direction toward?</u>

It is Never Too Late to Better Your Love's Fate!

<u>(End of the Introduction to Love Induction)</u>

To Master the Aching of the Heart, Become Overly Smart!

"Dance as if no one is watching, sing as if no one is listening, love as if no one had ever betrayed you, and live as if the Earth is the Heaven!" *(Mark Twain)*

Part One

Computer-Coding Demands Love-Re-Molding!

Start Creating the Storage of the Rainbow of Knowledge!

1. "The Whole of Life Lies in the Verb LOVING!" *(Teilhard de Chardin)*

Don't Be Love-Automatic;
Be Love Aristocratic!

Love is Not a Game;
It's the Life Gain!

2. Don't Love Automatically or Statically!

Don't love automatically,

Commonly, or statically,

Also, don't love sporadically,

And too emphatically!

Love continuously

And consciously!

Your immortal soul

Needs a conscious control!

It follows the lead of your thought

And then communicates it to the emotional fort.

Your soul talks to you through intuition

And protects you against the spirit's depletion!

If you love thoughtfully and dynamically,

Your life changes dramatically!

So, program yourself on the pulse,

Happy, happy, happy, thus,

And never reverse it into

Snappy, snappy, snappy fuss!

Only with light in your inner sight,

Is love full of unbeatable might!

Don't get into the Common Love Swings; Give Your Love Spiritual Wings!

3. Love Elation is in Self-Revelation!

We are evolving our intelligence to enrich our spirituality and to raise our self-consciousness. It should be done, not just in a religiously-mechanical way, but through deep, insightfully aware, unshakable knowing that we are being digitally governed from the Above, or, in fact, everywhere by some creative force - **The Universal Intelligence, the Master Mind, or the Source** that we all perceive as God.

"Man may produce the stumbling stones; God alone, in the mind of man may make them steppingstones." (Edgar Cayce)

I believe that every sacred book that I have is, actually, unfolding the secret of life in the five levels: **physica**l *(mini)*; **emotional** *(meta)*; **mental** *(mezzo)*; **spiritual**(*macro*). ;and *universal (super)*. We should all be developing **the Super-Conscious Mind** holistically and auto-suggestively. Our spiritual maturation is our inner elation!

Super level – **I perceive with my soul;** *and I see myself as part of the Whole!*

Macro level – **I acculturate,** *socialize, and spiritualize my life; I'm alive!*

Mezzo level – **I intellectualize** *and individualize myself in every cell!*

Meta level - **I emotionalize** *my mind and get more psychologically aware.*

Mini level - **I personalize** *myself mentally, physically, and verbally.*

The body is a *physical, emotional, mental, spiritual, and universal* conduit of the entire life in the Cosmos, and therefore, it needs to be sculptured in all these planes love-wise, too. Each level is integrated with the next one.

We call this union - **personal integrity**, and it manifests the outcome of the Self-Actualization process that is **love-impregnated** and that ends up with life itself. All religions are the interpretations of the eternal concept of creation. In his great book, *"The Stellar Man,* John Baines writes,"

"Spiritual Aristocracy begins with the Individual and Ends with Him."

4. Digital Transformation is in Self-Reformation!

At present, when we are in *the 3-D reality*, heading toward **5-D DIGITAL TRANSFORMATION,** we are sucked into the virtual reality more and more, but a very fragile border line between the reality and a personal growth should not be entirely broken.

Stop fun- crawling and lying, start growing and flying!

A self-resurrecting person should meet all the strains of modern civilization with a new fortified sense *of sane, well-balanced and consciously controlled life* in a holistically- structured way. Being a mother / father, or a great professional is not enough now. We all need **SELF-INSTALLATION** in life and **SELF-REALIZATION** of the unique talents that we are all granted with from the Above.

Without love as the permeating force in this growth, nothing can truly be accomplished because love cannot be put in the second place. Love ability is above any goals. It is called **LOVE INTUITION** - the feeling that needs to be learnt, nurtured, and developed in five steps.

1. Love Visualization
2. The Law of Attraction Activization
3. Reading of the Universal Signs
4. Filtration of Information
5. Love-Actualization

The route of the *love intuition formation* as the eternal wisdom of life and loving. should be passed to our kids, raised not in religious piety that they reject now, but in the sacredness of the grains of wisdom that the centuries of rich religious experience have instilled in us, transforming it naturally into **SPIRITUAL MATURITY** that at this level of technological transformation we must all acquire. So, let's accept love simulation with better awareness and no frustration!

To Love-Excel, Choreograph Yourself!

5. Souls Grow Stale from Love Routine! Don't Let it Spin!

Our technological reality is pushing us to a new mental projection of a **DIGITAL SELF.** This time is adding quality to quantity.

The era of simulation is entering our minds and hearts station!

We are not living in simulation of love yet, but we are moving in that direction. Simulated lives and love will merge with the reality that is programming our getting digitized minds through video games and the **3D** movies. **AVATAR LOVE** will soon rule in our hearts and minds in **5D**. The most predictable and fantastically made movies, such as *"Matrix"* and *"Her"* are great examples of simulation of our future reality, and their images are truly pervasive and mesmerizing. Soon games will become indistinguishable from the reality, and we cannot even predict how such digital invasion will affect our kids and their ability to love. When they are in simulation reality, they exist outside it, anyway, and our responsibility is to draw the line between the simulation and the reality to them, and of course, not fall into the virtual reality entirely ourselves. The old saying " *It takes a village to raise a child"* has a new meaning now.

It talks a smart phone to raise a child!

Obviously, we need to provide congenial conditions for *a personal growth of our kids*. We are not only their parents, we are their teachers of life and love, and we are their psychiatrists, able to save them from *the spinning vortex of limited love perception* that sucks them in very early and that is easily accessible on the smart phone. We need now to widen the scope of our interests in five levels and ten basic intelligences that I present in the book " *Living Intelligence or the Art of Becoming."-2019).*

There is no Self-Growing in just accumulating New Knowledge. It's in Conscious Using it!

6. Love Resurrection is in Love Intelligence Perfection!

Love is the means that defines the process of personal self-growth! To begin with, we need to build up the basis of the dilettante knowledge in the most vital realms of life. Any evolving ability is, in fact, based on **GENERAL INTELLIGENCE + LOVE INTELLIGENCE** - *mind and heart in sync* that we need to develop consciously in ourselves and our kids, sifting the information for its validity at every level of its reception in the five levels of **LOVE-RESURECTION.**

5. Universal level	*Self-Salvation*
4. Spiritual level	*Self-Realization*
3. Mental level	*Self-Installation*
2. Emotional level	*Self-Monitoring*
1. Physical level	*Self-Awareness*

All the stages are interconnected in the holistic system that is meant to develop our indispensable ability *<u>to trace every problem in life or love to the cause.</u>*

10. **Universal Intelligence**	**Super-Level** of Consciousness
9. **Spiritual Intelligence**	<u>(The Universal Dimension)</u>
8 **Social Intelligence**	**Macro- Level**
7. **Cultural Intelligence**	<u>(The Spiritual Dimension)</u>
6. **Financial Intelligence**	**Mezzo-Level**
5.**Professional** /*Creative* / **Intelligence**	<u>(The Mental Dimension)</u>
4. **Psychological Intelligence**	**Meta- Level**
3 **Emotional Intelligence**	<u>(The Emotional Dimension)</u> **Stage 3**
`2. **Language Intelligence**	**Mini-Level**
1. **General Intelligence**(*Self-Genesis*)	<u>(The Physical Dimension)</u>

Become a Holistically Developed, Love-Enhanced Self!

7. To Reach a New Love Site, Scan it with Your Inner Might!

The goal of life is to raise our self-consciousness and acquire the State of love from the Above, or to charge our minds and hearts, our magnetic center. of life action is in fraction.

Love is the unity of the heart and the mind in one electrical wind!

However, the know-how of this action is in fraction. We keep repeating senselessly" **God is Love,"** but we do not know how to generate the state of love in ourselves, keep it for years, and leave this world with the legacy of love, instilled in those who come after us. God, in fact, is the state of love from the Above, and <u>*the meaning of praying is in love-gaining.*</u> Our love gaining, however, has changed with the coming of the technological revolution. Inner sacredness and sincerity that are at the core of the state of love are now digitally charged, and we need to scan the sincerity and the authenticity of the other side's love might in five dimensions, too. The essence of *praying is becoming more and more viral in this respect,* transforming our working at bettering ourselves into the virtual reality of simulation that enhances and energizes this process with a spiritual might in others, too..

Love Simulation is teaching us spiritual love ration!

Praying is no longer a dead religious ritual of automatic reciting of the Bible and church instilled maxima. Praying is becoming more conscious, meditative, and self-reflective. <u>**Praying is a new method of Self-Resurrection with a digital self-reflection!**</u> The accessibility to the sacred books, beautiful talks, communicated by the truly Godly people like Sadhguru, Joel Osteen, many advanced thinking priests, scientists, and other accomplished people who share their wisdom on the Internet, enriches our intelligence and expands our perception of life and love as a new technologically- enhanced stuff..

Develop the Mind + Heart Might with the Love Channeling Sight!

8. Place Your Love Realms on the New Awareness Stems!

Many meditative practices, among which I personally favor the ***Transcendental Meditation** by Dr. John Hagelin,* involve us into another, much more sacred train of thought at just a click of a finger.

Undoubtedly, our *spiritual maturity* is growing by the day, and even though love relationships are often monitored by the exaggeration of the participants' personal values on different match sites, the possibilities of finding love have become infinite.

So, take a while and welcome love with a smile!

But learn to sift the information in the holistic love ration. Process your scanning of love suitors through *the universal, spiritual, mental, emotional, and physical X-raying.* Wisdom is multi-dimensional, too.

Every one of us is either a clear vessel of light, or a stuffed vessel that needs cleaning.*"(Edgar Cayce)*

Thus, the search of love will be governed from the Above. Mind it, please, that it should not start *at the physical level*, develop somewhat **at the emotional one**, get a little probed **at the *metal level,*** and most certainly, stop *at the spiritual one*.

It's worth waiting and love prorating, starting with the top of the holistic pyramid of self-growth and coming to its love-enhanced conclusion!

<u>*Help the love boot start walking on the Universal Route!*</u>

"Go Beyond, Fully Beyond, Completely Beyond!"

(The Buddhist Mantra)

Don't be Terrestrially Reactive;
Be Extra-Terrestrially Proactive!

9. Love Oasis Grows First on the Social Basis!

Life proves that we are social beings Our values and love aspirations are mostly affected not by the family and a great love example of the parents or grandparents, but they are shaped by the society, school, mass media, a group of friends, and the social trends. *Mark Averell* writes in this respect,

" ***Don't be afraid of death, be afraid of never start living!***"

Whatever the social system - *capitalism or socialism*, with one, having plenty, but characterized by soul depletion, and the other, having little, but demonstrating more soul richness, we are still dealing with being **GODLY** in a **GODLESS WORLD.** In the socialist atheistic society that I came from, many churches were turned into the storage places after the revolution of 1917, and mostly old people frequented the churches that were left intact. I remember my mom urging me and my younger brother to go to church with her,

" ***Remember, socialism is not forever, God is!***"

However, people in the former Soviet Union were very friendly and fraternal in spirit, very intelligence-oriented, always surrounded by books and looking with admiration at the people on the other side of *"the iron curtain, "* striving to immigrate to the world of freedom. Once we did immigrate, the world of freedom surprised us with the churches at every corner, but a very impersonal attitude of people to each other, discrimination of the immigrants and black Americans((*not in word, but in action*), and very materialistic souls.

Love Fort is now at the mercy of Money God!

However, here, I feel my belonging to the global international community of *the citizens of the world* in their **FRACTAL INDIVIDUALITY,** irrespective of the space and time they are in.

" *Time is not Money; Time is Life!*"

10. Soul-Refining is in Self-Redefining!

We all feel the presence of the Universal Intelligence and its impact on our lives. Our mind is evolving together with the Mind Above. ***Life is not a virtual game, or a rehearsal;*** it's a logical, eternal, and electromagnetic expression of love that brought us to Earth, to begin with. ***But we get bored in the ever-lasting love bliss!*** Love is not our goal, it is not the main stimulus in the evolution of our self-growth that is going on holistically in the ***physical, emotional, mental, spiritual, and universal realms.*** I might be wrong in seeing some things, but what I am sure of is <u>***the objectivity of the knowledge***</u> that I present here. We must not be focused on anyone's subjective opinions. Time is changing us exponentially and the old knowledge becomes obscene.

<u>*We all, like A. Einstein, should probe the realm of God's thought.*</u>

Unfortunately, we disregard the fact that love plays the most significant role in every sphere of our life because we are successful in any undertaking if we *"put much love into it."* Love enhances the creativity and, most importantly, ***it boosts the spirit*** that plays the pivotal role in the ***mind + heart*** unity. *"Your body is your spirit!" (Jeffrey Allen)*

<u>**MIND + SPIRIT + HEART + SELF-CONSCIOUSNESS + SUPER-CONSCIOUSNESS**</u> = **The Soul-Refined You!**

Vector of time / Mind development

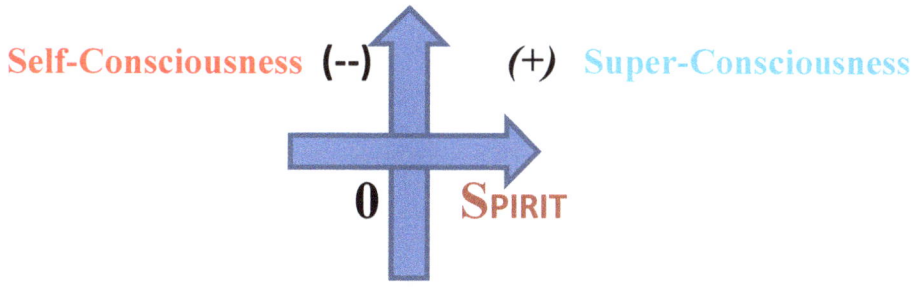

Self-Consciousness **(--)**   **(+)** Super-Consciousness

0   S<small>PIRIT</small>

Vector of Space / Body development

𝒯𝒽𝑒 𝒯𝓇𝒾𝓊𝓂𝓅𝒽 𝑜𝒻 𝓉𝒽𝑒 𝑀𝒾𝓃𝒹 𝑜𝓋𝑒𝓇 𝓉𝒽𝑒 𝐵𝑜𝒹𝓎 𝒾𝓈 𝒪𝓊𝓇 𝒰𝓃𝒾𝓋𝑒𝓇𝓈𝒶𝓁 𝒢𝓁𝑜𝓇𝓎!

11. Place Your Love Realms on the New Awareness Stems!

For centuries on end, the humanity has been striving to survive all kinds of life challenges and tribulations. ***The time has come to learn to live and to thrive, not just to survive.*** The goal to create an ideal man in life is the goal of the Universe in its creative strife! New times - new perception of life and love! Love has become our mission for the God's admission!

<u>The Form + Content of life are beyond the common drive!</u>

The concept of love is obtaining a new definition because love is the core of our growing self-consciousness. We are igniting it technologically now through the spirit that is infinite!

It's the universal phenomenon now, the evolutionary restoration of the **MIND + HEART** *link formation.*

The search for love is at a high tide. Inevitably, the foam of the dirty thinking and feeling will eventually subside aside, and we'll learn to trust love back, or to sincerely love and be loved in return.

To have love, give love to those here and Above!

However, *o*ur evolutionary transformation requires the change of the old **LOVE HAVITS** and instilling of the new **LOVE SKILLS**. The first should be formed from birth, the second must be **SELF-INSTALLED** throughout the entire lifetime in five levels of self-resurrection: *physical, emotional, mental, spiritual, and universal*.

The love in time and space is at the technological life's base!

It means that <u>we should change the **FORM** and **CONTENT** of the life we live.</u> Changing ourselves in time and in the inner and outer space of life is the demand of the evolution and our ultimate life's solution! *Dr. Fred Bell – in his wonderfully informative book book " Rays of Truth -Crystal of Light", reminds us,*

"Life is Not a Circle; It's a Spiral!"

12. Evolution vs. Stagnation is at the Core of the Technological Elation!

It's vital now that we start analyzing the **CAUSE-EFFECT** disconnection *between our thinking, speaking, feeling and acting, or between the heart and the mind. We know it, but we are not aware of it*! <u>Awareness is informed attention,</u> and it needs to be paid to every thought, word, feeling, or action that we generate to reason out the consequences of our mindless living and loving that we have to face in time and space, paying for the consequences of our mindlessness.

The consequences of our actions envision is the best life's provision!

Life awareness demands changing the circle of people that you communicate with, quitting a routine job, breaking the unhealthy friendships and partnerships, and stopping the internship of negativity and lying, using the justifiable comment, "*No one is perfect!*"

<u>**But love is as much the way of thinking as it is the way of feeling!**</u>

Love is an evolutionary phenomenon as everything else around us, and **we shouldn't let the dirty fun generate the soul's scum**! We need to stop tolerating the negative talking, feelings, and actions of other people as well as the mass media programming. We shouldn't allow the poisonous impact ruin our own and the kids' psyche. Not to let the emotional chaos mar the mind's heaven, we need *to synchronize the form and the content* of our lives consciously and continuously.

Discipline yourself to beat the Evil Inner Spell!

Form + **Content**

(Body+ Spirit+ Mind) + (Self-Consciousness + Universal Consciousness) = *The Whole Self!*

Taking Care of the Inner Dialog's Mystics forms Our Life's Logistics!

13. The Channels of Your Perception are Cleaned by an Aware Reception!

Everyone is blessed with Love from the Above, but we need to tune ourselves out of the vibrations of discontent and hate that other people emit, too. We often generate a lower level of vibrations than the situation that we are in, and such situation generates a lot of problems. The lower you sink in your vibrations, or someone else's, the weaker your willpower will be. ***Learn to resist and reform the evil de-form!***

In each problematic situation, step back or step aside and look at it from a bird's eye view. Read the universal signs, decipher the coincidences, and focus on the **LOVE GRAVITY** in your center of love from the Above. The channels of perception must be radically cleaned by you. Your perception of life would change if you re-direct your aware attention from the physical perception of the world to first *universal, spiritual, mental, emotional,* and, finally, *the physical one.*

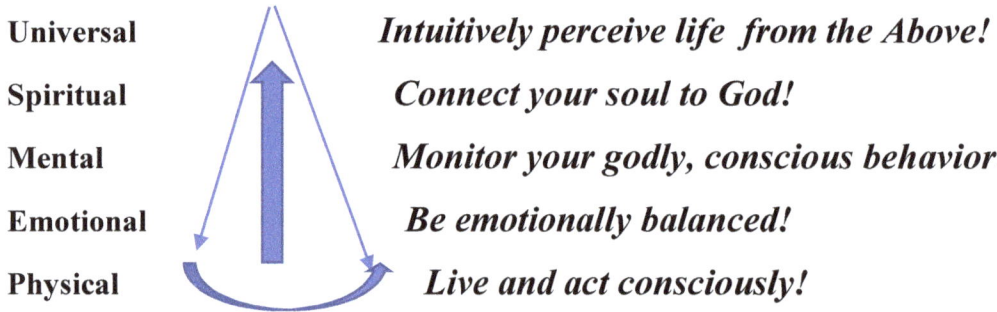

Universal	*Intuitively perceive life from the Above!*
Spiritual	*Connect your soul to God!*
Mental	*Monitor your godly, conscious behavior!*
Emotional	*Be emotionally balanced!*
Physical	*Live and act consciously!*

Our acting in life, in general, and in love situation, in particular, has now a reverse direction that multiplies our problems and testifies to our *spiritual immaturity.*

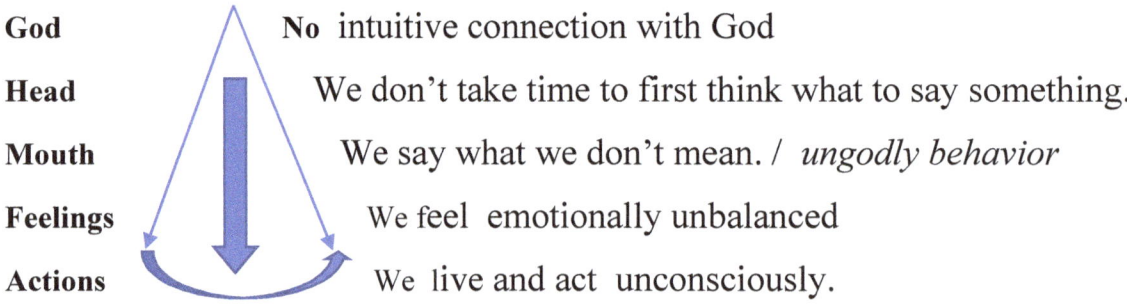

God	No intuitive connection with God
Head	We don't take time to first think what to say something.
Mouth	We say what we don't mean. / *ungodly behavior*
Feelings	We feel emotionally unbalanced
Actions	We live and act unconsciously.

As People Treat You and You Treat Them, so Does God!

14. Self-Enlightenment

(An Inspirational Booster)

Try to find beauty in ordinary things
That are around us in strings.
   The string theory of matter
    Presents beauty in every gutter!
The beauty is everywhere,
It's in the ugly and fair!
   Just adjust your vision
    To seeing the invisible beauty provision,
And unite it as One
With the Universal energy + information fun!
   Thus, you'll make a leap
    From virtual potentiality to life actuality!
You'll unfold yourself in stride
To the Luminosity of Life!

All serious daring starts with the beauty within!

"The purpose of life is the perfection of character."

(*Yamada Roshi / Zen philosophy*)

Enlightenment is Being One with the Entirety of the New Living Fun!

(End of Part One - Computer Coding in Love Molding)

As Part of Nature, We fractalize Our Inner Structure.

The Love Sparks of Each of Us are in the Formation of the Soul's Mass!

Part Two

The Know-How of Living in Five Dimensions of Being

Love

Fractals

There is no System without the Structure!

The Pyramid of Self-Growth to Consider:

5. Universal dimension   ***Self-Salvation***
4. Spiritual dimension   ***Self-Realization***
3. Mental dimension   ***Self-Installation***
2. Emotional dimension   ***Self-Monitoring***
1. Physical dimension   ***Self-Awareness***

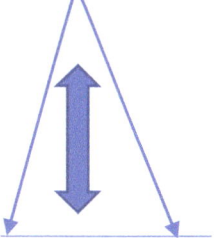

To Be Love Inspired, Be Self-Inspiringly Revised and Rewired!

1. Don't Let Your Life Just Happen!

Channel Your Living Through NEW Thinking, Feeling, and SEEING; Become the Time-Reformed BEING!

Release the drops of kindness with love mindfulness!

Charge Your Virtually Impacted Life with a Consciously Steered Drive!

2. Love Fractals are the Life Functional Matters.

In the previous five books on Self-Resurrection, I have introduced my vision of *the fractals of self-creation* that we need to focus on forming at this technologically overwhelming time. The reference is made to a great discovery of the fractals in nature by **Dr. Benoit Mandelbrot** (*Check out the book " I Am Free to Be the Best of Me!"*) Here, I accentuate the sacred direction of love from the Above that, in my vision, will last through the tribulations of life if it is holistically perceived and constantly X-rayed in five dimensions of conscious living and loving.

The direction of love from the Above goes in levels:

Level	
Universal	Intuitively perceive love from the Above
Spiritual	Connect your soul to God
Mental	Say what you mean / **Godly, conscious behavior**
Emotional	Be emotionally balanced and life aware
Physical	Love consciously and morally

Become more reflective on your love life that needs your *aware attention* to form a healthy, time-sustaining **FRACTAL OF LOVE**.

Fractals of Spiritualized Love:

Form + *Content*

(Body+ Spirit+ Mind) + (Self-Consciousness + Universal Consciousness)

Living Intelligence + *Enlightened Self-Consciousness = A Whole Self!*

Read the part of the book "*For the Reader to Consider*" or skip it around. Give *the auto-inducive nature of the book* time to work You might discover the glimpse of the magic that we all call **LOVE**.

Simplify life, simplify, simplify to get to the God's WY-5!

Don't Be Blind in the Heart; Be Virtually Smart!

3. Love Gravity is Formed by the Fractals of Self-Symmetry!

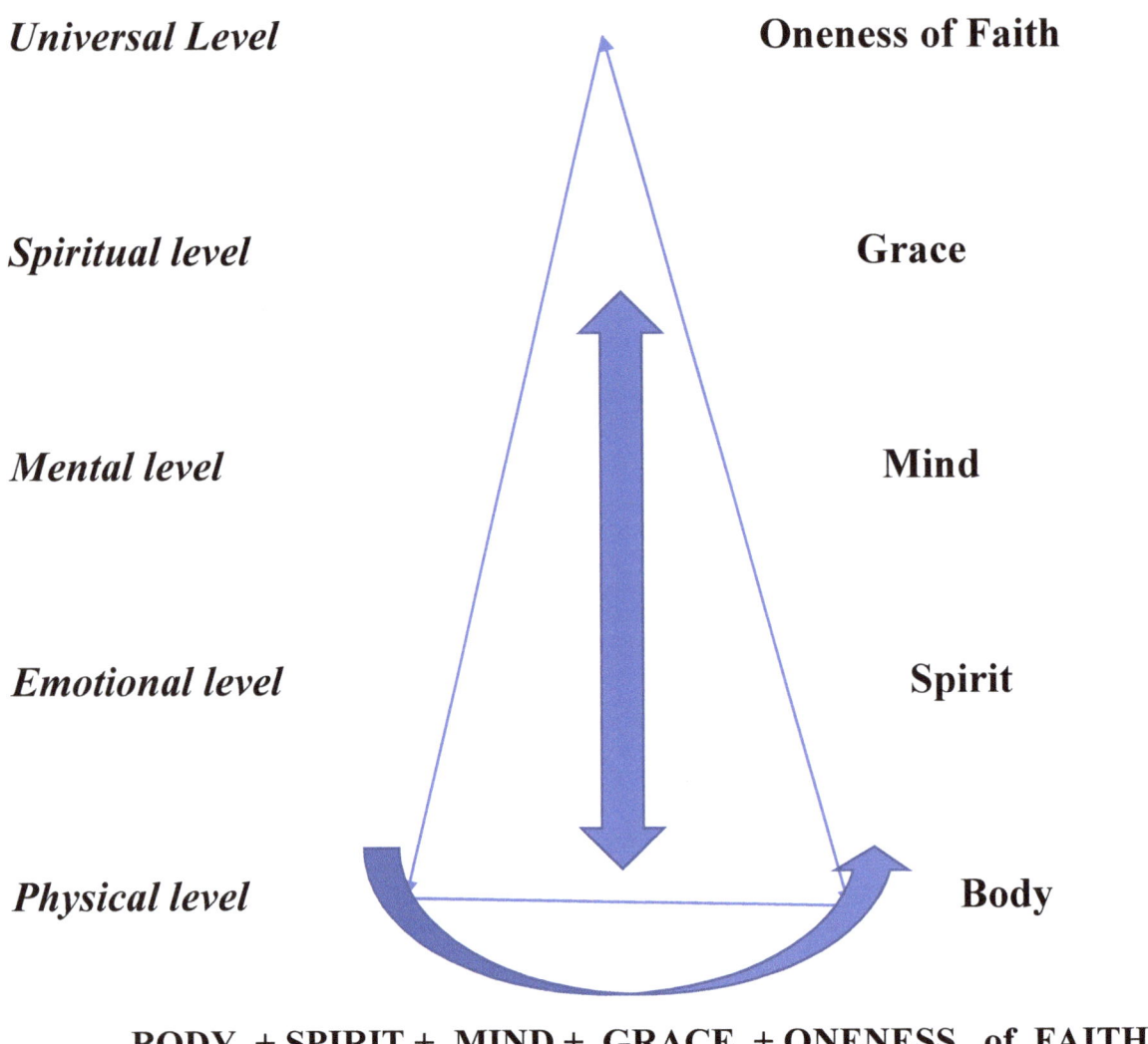

Universal Level	Oneness of Faith
Spiritual level	Grace
Mental level	Mind
Emotional level	Spirit
Physical level	Body

BODY + SPIRIT + MIND + GRACE + ONENESS of FAITH!

= Love - Gravity!

Flood your body with higher consciousness in the morning and before going to bed. <u>Help your love be consciously fed!</u>

Let's Live and Love
By the Eternal Symmetry of Love!

4. Love Creation is in Inner Illumination

"Life is a dance of time and space. The beauty of life is in keeping the rhythm of this dance." (Sadhguru) Every generation has its own rhythm of love, but the essential self-constructive and inspirational values of love never change.

The Ingredients of Love-Growth are in our Fractal Souls!

Mind

Vector of Time / **Mind development**

Self-Consciousness (-)   **(+) Super-Consciousness**

0 *Spirit*

Vector of Space / **Body development**

Body

The Spirit is Our Life-Energizer and Life-Actualizer!

Form + **Content**

(Body+ Spirit+ Mind) + (Self-Consciousness + Universal Consciousness)

= A Love Fractal

The Form + Content of a Love Cell Build up the Whole Love-Sealed Self!

5. We are One in Love, and Love is One in Us!

We are part of *the Universal Flow of Love*, and if you start perceiving yourself as an **ETERNAL SOUL,** but not as a separate personage of life, you will make the right turn toward self-reliance, self-sufficiency, and self-love. *Love in essentially double-directional*. On the one hand, love helps us become more self-aware, on the other one, love unites two minds and hearts into a long-lasting united soul's flight.

Love is glued by the sense of belonging to each other!

The people that love each other become *an integral fractal of life* that is totally and irreversibly alive! Each partner is no longer a person who plays his part in the performance of life in which every role is scripted. He is the **MASTER OF HIS LIFE**, and he makes the choices where to channel it. In this way, love activates *the genetic code of the divine unity* in a couple that with a birth of a child becomes the **TRINITY OF LOVE**. True love helps us become *unique selves* consciously. *Love individualizes and personalizes,* and that's the main reason people like to get married! They unite the time and space of their lives but remain separate fractals of love.

The Fractal of a Spiritualized Love:

Form + *Content*

(Body+ Spirit+ Mind) + (Self-Consciousness + Universal Consciousness)

Living Intelligence + *Enlightened Self-Consciousness = A Whole Self!*

Surprisingly, many people now realize the responsibility for their own lives at the age of fifty, or even sixty - the age of wisdom. But why not **ENJOY the AUTHENTICITY** of life and love at a much younger age, enlightened by the digital transformation of the humanity.

The Choices we make Dictate the Life we Live!

6. Deep Love Discontent Wakes up a Personal Intent!

The people that wake up for self-transformation have lived regular lives of the society programmed lives. They have been just husband / wives, successful / unsuccessful professionals, happy / unhappy parents, etc., but they inwardly have never accepted the flow of their limited lives.

Stagnation cannot be the source of love elation!

Discontent with life and love de-magnetize **the common gravity** of the couple, and each partner starts feeling insecure in life, thinking wrongly that a new love relationship, an exciting love fling, or a new family will return the lost sense of gravity back. It never happens because there was no growth in the relationship in five dimensions of love and faith, confidence, compassion, and grace.

So, stop the undercurrent emotional disease. Detect the cause of your love unease and eliminate the freeze!

That's why being limited in self-expression is a more common reason for divorces than cheating that is often generated by the absence of understanding and support of the individual aspirations. People in love must **unite their personal goals into a common one** that needs to be reached from two different directions but channeled by a common course of *the place of love destination and solid gravity of belonging.*

Raising kids is not a common goal, it's just a common responsibility!

In sum, love helps people of any age reverse their lives, and it appears that age has nothing to do with the regular scenario of a commonly programmed life. ***When you know better, you live and love better!*** Consciously processed new information energizes us for change and helps us live and love again. This is when we can honestly declare,

I've Made a V-turn; I Love my Life, and Life Loves me in Return!

7. New Stuff is in the Code of Love!

We live on the phenomenal planet that is governed by *the emotional energy of love*, and it is unique in the space which is predominantly mental, and our growing in it makes a great difference.

Charismatic, spiral changes expand our life's ranges!

The breath of love was blown into us by Jesus Christ that planted the ***Philosophy of Love*** on Earth for us to be able to experience love, starting from the Above. According to Neuroscience, ***love has a neurological basis***. The scientists prove that when the neurotransmitter of love, called ***dopamine,*** is released in the brain, it contributes to a rise in energy, motivation, and feelings of euphoria or elation.

Love is hardwired into the structure of the human brain, not the heart
Isn't that a great fact?

From the spiritual point of view, ***I believe that love has a structural nature,*** too. In my understanding, it should be grown in five levels- ***physical, emotional, mental, spiritual, and universal*** our entire life, and this process needs to be backed up with the best pieces of art, literature, poetry, classical music, favorite melodies, movies, and any other activities that expand the knowledge horizons and make the nobility of the soul our life's main goal! This is how we should raise our kids. Then the dirty foam of quick-fix relationships and cool getting laid that is later shared with the other primitive seekers of pleasure as a great victory or the expression of manhood will be resisted by them consciously and the romantic essence of love will enlighten their hearts.

So, if love starts *on the **physical level***, it can or cannot ***grow emotionally.*** If it passed this level, it'll grow up to ***the emotional / psychological level*** of mutual understanding. It becomes much stronger, but it is still not enough for the love emotion to last. ***It needs the mental back-up*** – the connection on the intellectual level.

Then, we'll get a New Love's Vision with a Better Precision!

8. The Job of Love is the Eternal Stuff!

According to Edgar Cayce, the two loving people need to have" *the union of purpose"* in life. If love has sustained the growth in the three levels, mentioned above, it is prone to die eventually, anyway, because *there is no spiritual connection* in it. Therefore, people from different religious backgrounds can hardly keep their love alive for long.

Only love, *processed through all the levels* accumulates strength to last for years on end! Sometimes, in the luckiest cases, people scan each other in five levels during the first, second date and their clicking on all the levels glues them together or years, if not the entire life. *They have ripened spiritually*, and the soul mates get magnetized to a mutually sewed love then and there.

The trajectory of love must be directed from the Above!

That is why *a one-night stand* or a love relationship that is based just on the physical spark cannot last. It's doomed to get demagnetized if the partners do not get wise. Like anything else in life, love must grow together with a person's intelligence and self-consciousness, and it is much better if it gets sparked up *at the spiritual level first*, gravitates to the *intellectual* connection, connects at the heart's level *emotionally,* and culminates in a passionate *love crescendo* physically.

Even the love of God is not just granted, it's earned!

Such love relationship is <u>*heart + mind*</u> based, and it grows to be endless! In sum, you cannot become a loving person if you didn't program yourself for being one!

Dear God! Throw me a handful of stars

And bless me with love

From the Above!

Love Creation is in Our Inner Illumination!

9. To Connect to a New Love Wi-Fi, Follow the route of What, How, and Why.

The new wave of light is approaching the Earth now, and we are entering the expedient time of soul transformation. ***New information generates new neuron connections in the brain.*** We become stronger when we think consciously, when we sift the up-coming information for its validity, and when we **auto-suggestively re-program the mind.** We see the reality differently; we are becoming much more self-aware!

(Global warming and sex emancipation in time ration.)

People are "***love-lazy***" now. They want love to happen to them. Dr. Paul Pearsall calls it **the "*Cupid Complex*"**. He writes, " *People are passively waiting for an arrow of love to strike, rather than acting lovingly to be a cupid themselves.*" Tune your **AUTO-ANTENNA** to the Universal Love Station and analyze your love frustration by the holistic paradigm's ration - ***Synthesis-Analysis-Synthesis!***

Generalize - Analyze - Actualize!

Love Flows through the Time and Space to the Highest Integrity Base!

10. We Need to Live in Line with the Space-Time Twine!

As is indicated above, we are evolving not on the physiological level of adaptation to the life in the Universe, but *on its holistic scene* – in the *physical, emotional, mental, spiritual, and universal* dimensions of our inner and outer life. Love is the energy of creation that is generating the **WISDOM OF CREATION** in us. It is supposed to result into *love for all life* and respect for its sacred expression in any form

"Spirituality is not a disability; it is a phenomenal empowerment of life." (Sadhguru)

Our creative curiosity is enticed by the spiritual energy that we are overwhelmingly surrounded with, and it is charged by the energy of the spirit. Curiosity is driving the wisdom of creation, developing its utmost product –***"the creative imagination"*** *(Carl Yung)*, whetted now by the technologically enhanced visualization.

Our spiritual maturation is, in fact, our *self-growth in the physical, emotional mental, spiritual, and universal realms of life,* backed up by the sync of the **MIND+ HEART** connection. The unity of the heart and the mind, ***not just the genitals,*** remains at the core of our evolutionary self-transformation that everyone is experiencing now.

Self-growth is not the change of sex-orientation. It is everyone's personal search for love that should not be viewed as a deviation from the "norm, geared by mass media to a new definition of love – ***a dirty self-expression in public.*** It surely sells, but it doesn't return to love its sacredness as the most powerful energy of two minds and hearts' common beat in its mentally- emotional vault! If any inner discomfort resides in your heart, start searching the reason for it in the mind. *"If your heart is wise, my heart will rejoice." (Proverbs 23,15*

The Universal Love Source is focused on Our Self-Growth Force!

11. The Anatomy of Love Knowledge in the Universal Storage!

Work on Your Love Goal by the Self-Growth Pole!

Synthesis - Analysis – Synthesis

or

Generalize – Internalize – Personalize!

(For more on this paradigm, check out the book "Self-Taming!")

Constantly process your love through the holistic paradigm of life - in the physical, emotional, mental, spiritual, and universal dimensions of you and your partner's love reflections.

Don't Take Love for Granted; It is God Granted!

Expand Your Love Range and Consciously Change!

(Pictures by Yolanta Lensky)

My Solar System is My Fate, and It's Great!

Part Three - Book Structure

(The Main Parts of the Book in the Mind's Nook)

Love Zones

(In five dimensions: Physical, Emotional, Mental, Spiritual, and Universal))

The Structure of a Book determines the Depth of its Mind's Nook!

1. The Growth of Love Starts from the Above!

Move from a negative love eruption to the Spiritual Love dimension!

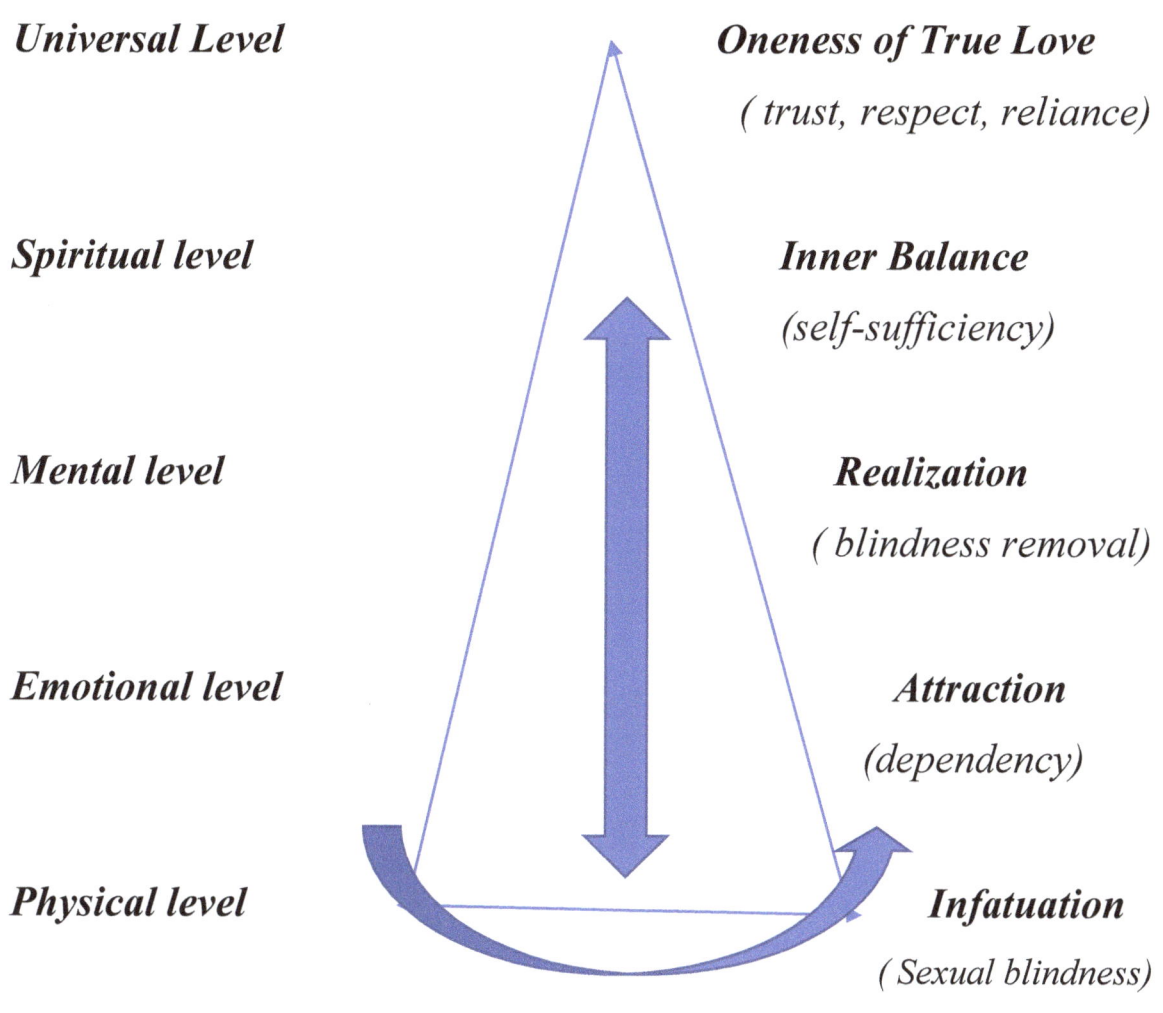

Universal Level	**Oneness of True Love** (trust, respect, reliance)
Spiritual level	**Inner Balance** (self-sufficiency)
Mental level	**Realization** (blindness removal)
Emotional level	**Attraction** (dependency)
Physical level	**Infatuation** (Sexual blindness)

Love is Our Perpetua Mobile!

To Be Decent and Gifted at the Same Time; Be Self-Refined!

Harmony is Me; Harmony is My Love Philosophy!

2. Love Myth is the Multi-Dimensional Bliss!

Trace the of **Self-Growth Pyramid** at the beginning of this book with **the Paradigm of Love**, presented here in five dimensions, too! Each level is featured in its essential standpoints as the main parts of the book below. Expand your vision with an insightful love provision.

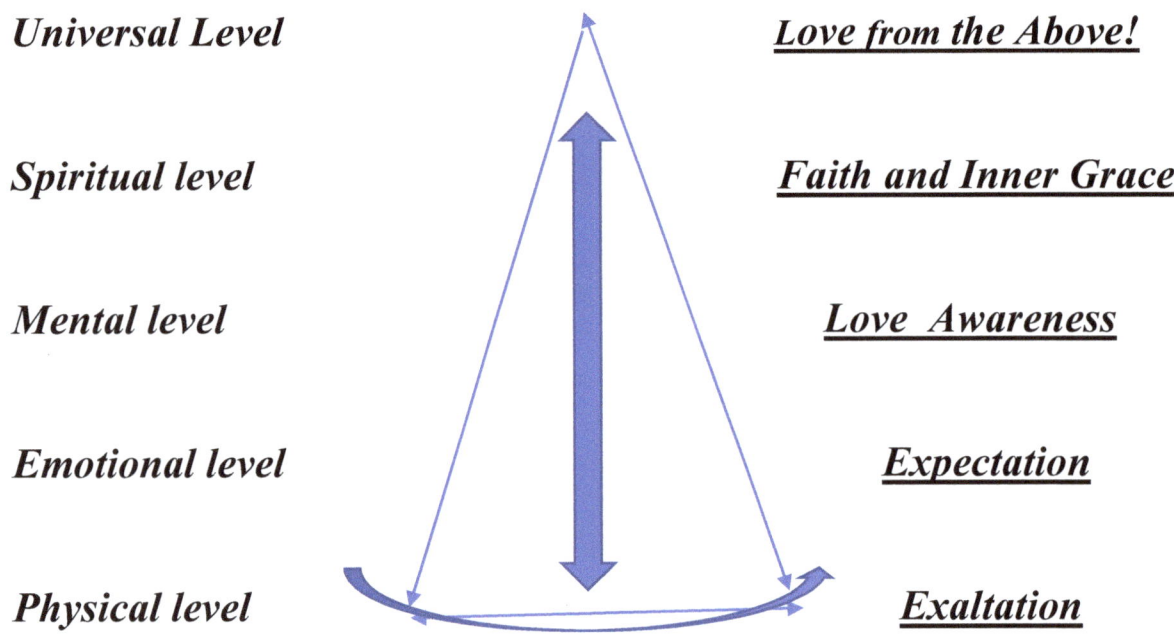

Universal Level	*Love from the Above!*
Spiritual level	*Faith and Inner Grace*
Mental level	*Love Awareness*
Emotional level	*Expectation*
Physical level	*Exaltation*

The Zones of Love from the Above:

The Main Parts of the Book:

5. **Universal Level** – *Oneness and Inner Sacredness* - **Love Bliss Zone**
4. **Spiritual Level** - *Faith and Inner Grace* – **Self-Sufficiency Zone**
3. **Mental Level** – *Self-Love* - **Love Awareness Zone**
2. **Emotional Level** – *Expectation /Justification* – **Breach of Trust Zone**
1. **Physical Level** - *Exaltation and Love Elation.* - **Risk Zone**

To Charge Your Love Force is the Hardest Job on Earth!

3. Shape Your Life's Mold by a Personally Devised Love Code!

To begin with, every one of us starts life with taking the risk in *the Risk Zone of Love* with which I start featuring each level of the **HOLISTIC LOVE EDUCATION**, one by one below.

Love is the greatest reflection of a person's self-perfection!

To conquer the negative emotions in love, stop depending on your friends' advice and the events outside of you devise the love code that you want to work out for yourself in the *physical, emotional, mental, spiritual, and universal* realms of life. You will find some helpful ones below.

Incentivize your inner love stuff with the Codes of Love!

In the *Book Incentive section*, I have mentioned that this book presents all the chunks of well sifted information as the **CODES OF LOVE** in five essential dimensions of love and in each of the love zones, featured consequentially next. Below, there are thirty-five different codes of love that I offer for your consideration, *as the auto-suggestive inductions.* The titles of all chunks of information in this book and the mind-sets, concluding them, *rhyme to make the brain love coding* simpler and more memorable. These rhyming, mentally emotional mind-sets are meant to play the role of self-conducted **LOVE THERAPY** and each of them presents an array of love codes, too.

You can easily upload them to your smart phone and have them at hand as *a self-help reminder* at the time of your sagging love mood. Pick the ones you like most, add your own ones, and upload the ones that are working for you at the moment. They will help you in your **LOVE MATURATION** and protect you from love frustration.

Enrich your Love Horizon with your Own Love Codes Devising!

4. The Auto-Suggestive Love-Coding for Life-Molding

1. Life is not a circle, it's of a spiral range! **CHANGE!**

2. Live and love while you are alive!

3. Unearth your love emotions with pride!

4. Love cannot be politically correct; love is politically inept!

5. <u>Love exists in time and space only with Grace!</u>

6. Spiritual immaturity ruins love's heart + mind unity!

7. Love is not an obligation. it's a love relation!

8. To stop the love aching of the heart, be overly smart!

9. Live and love without any bluff!

10. <u>No lying, cheating, gambling, drinking, fighting, and money prioritizing. Do more love wising!</u>

11. If you have a major crush on someone, keep it from the public's smothering tongue.

12. Be self-wising. Don't allow your love patronizing!

13. Don't drown love in profanity and self-vanity!

14. Don't have excuses for any insults and abuses!

15. Don't reject before being rejected!

16. Don't exaggerate rejection, don't fall apart, be smart!

17. Don't be domineering; be more considering!

18. <u>Love is not a slave. Don't put it in a cave!</u>

19. If you have a dispute, it's wiser to zip your mouth and listen to the other.

20. Sincerity is the virtue of divinity!

<u>21. Always say what you mean and mean what you say not to let your love sway away!</u>

22. To be edgy and sharp in love kills its fragile stuff!

23. For love to last, find someone better than you fast!

24. There is no battle strategy that doesn't do love-damaging! War and love are the incompatible stuff!

<u>25. Meeting a person halfway is the love's way!</u>

26. Love is not demanding; it's granting!

27. Cheating is soul- twisting and love-resisting!

28. Don't stigmatize yourself with second standards, lying, cheating, and whining!

29. Forgiving is hard, but it damages you more than that!

<u>30. Do not abandon your mate in any state!</u>

31. Love lasts if you do not live fast!

32. The sense of measure is a great treasure!

33. Don't Love and Run, Strategize Your Love for Years to come!

34. Let the final stop for the two of Thee in the love life's rein be the birch tree on your common grave!

35. Keep repeating auto-suggestively,

<u>I can Roam any Terrain with Love in My Vein!</u> etc.

In the Universal Love Code, Each of Us has an Individual Mold!

5. Carpe Diem! Seize the Day! There is No Time for Delay!

Love is a Miracle That You can't stop with a Sigh; Long Live the Amplitude You Either Fall, or Fly!

Don't Expect Love, Give it!

(End of the Book Structure Part Three)

For Love to Happen, Learn to Love Consciously!

(Mark Chagall)

The Physical Level of Love Creation is Not the First One in Love Elation!

Love Zone One

(Physical Dimension)

The Risk Zone

Exaltation and Love Elation

(The Self-Growth Level of Self-Awareness)

Form Your Love Salvation Link with Heart + Mind in Sync!

1. To Have Love, Be Love!

Internalize Your Emotions and Externalize the Mind; Be One of a Kind!

"It's Not Enough to Be the Best; Be the Only!" (Steve Jobs)

2. Love is Always an Equation!

(An Inspirational Booster)

Love is always an equation,

Either you love yourself more,

Or the object of an emotional invasion!

    The question" <u>Who is Who?</u>

    Remains a ruling sexual guru!

Either you control me, or I control you-

That is the power of " Who?"

    We never forestall

    The fight for the control.

It directs, it invades,

 And it inwardly breaks!

    It is a disease

    Of a de-magnetized " Is!"

Only the unity of you and me

Constitutes the whole without a selfish glee.

    So, tap into each other's interface

    To have an unbreakable love faith!

Grow into each other's space

But don't occupy it with the Ego's maze!

    The trunk of the Love's Tree

    Consists of the two parts - <u>You and Me!</u>

Minus and plus

Make real love, thus !

    They are inseparable and unbeatable,

        But their love is remittable.

You remit Me, and I remit You,

We are our common love's guru!

Our emotional health

Shouldn't be any shrink's wealth!

    We are both in charge to recharge

        Our unified cell to love-excel!

And we can monitor our common soul

To love-console!

    <u>*Marriage is an inspired decision,*</u>

        <u>*Made with precision*</u>*!*

The two hearts beat like One

only in the space and time of love!

Are You Spiritually Fit for the Marriage Love Beat?

3. Love is a Partnership with God!

(Auto-induction for Love-Function):

I am a Part of the Universe;

I'm the Divine Force!

We are of One Love Matter,

I am God's Partner!

Love is Freedom in Time and Space.
Love is Your Inner Grace!

4. Love's Security is in Our Spiritual Maturity!

In the section of the book *"For the Reader to First Consider,"* I have indicated that each book, presented in the holistic paradigm features consequentially *five stages of self - modifying and love coding* in the *physical, emotional, mental, spiritual, and universal realm as:*

LOVE -AWARENESS (*Physical level*) ; **LOVE -MONITORING** (*Emotional level*);
LOVE -INSTALLATION (*Mental level*) ; **LOVE -REALIZATION** (*Spiritual level*)
LOVE -SALVATION (*Universal level*). They are presented below as **love zones.**

Each book, in the emotional section of its conceptual structure, talks about love as the core element of our *mentally-emotional fitness*, calling on us to establish the essential **MIND+HEART** link – the basis of the Love from the Above.

Having already topped the holistic Self-Resurrection pyramid with the book *"Beyond the Terrestrial"* that features the universal dimension that we are technologically tapping into now, I decided to accentuate love importance separately as the phenomenon that incorporates all five levels of self-growth at the technologically wonderous times.

We are now on the go; we are in the Universal Love Flow!

It means that we need to live in harmony with ourselves and the outside world, especially if love betrays us and fails our expectations. Many suicides were committed due to love disillusionment, starting with the unforgettable story of the sincerest love of Romeo and Juliet.

I suggest analyzing the taste of the ***physical, emotional, mental, spiritual, and universal components of love*** on the holistic scene. My vision is very simple, and it is inspired with the idea that the **BEST MOMENT IS NOW**, and *Now is always filled with love expectations.* Unfortunately, our love relationships have grown stale and grey from the everyday routine and an impersonal attitude to each other.

To Master Love's Devine Stuff, Go by Your Own Code of Love!

5. Love Intelligence without Negligence

I have mentioned above that this book is not an attempt to moralize about love, its sinful manifestations, and human relationships, driven by emotions of sex-addiction, money-chasing, and fun-life glazing. Zillions of books are devoted to these topics, and in many cases, sincere love situations are substituted by spicy sex scenes. Many books are focused on **enticing the readers' sex energy**, instead of instilling in their souls the sacred feeling of love from the Above, the love that unifies, not divides.

Love making has overpowered authentic love-rating!

Processing your **LOVE INTELLIGENCE** through five levels of love growth will help me instill in your soul the inspirational energy for the most fantastic feeling of love, universal and self-inspiring. in its godly core.

Induct yourself with love at every stage of your life!

The five love levels are presented here consequentially as five love zones that you can see in the holistic pyramid. The principle of the **SPIRAL LOVE GROWTH** is observed here as,

Two steps forward, one step back – that's the present-day love track!

The technological revolution has sped up this process incredibly. Technology helps us realize that the authenticity of our emotions, even though they can be duplicated in robots, will still help us retain our *emotional superiority* through the unbreakable unity of our eternally *fractal connection of love,* monitored by our holistic self-growth.

MIND + SPIRIT + HEART + SELF-CONSCIOUSNESS + SUPER-CONSCIOUSNESS = The Soul-Refined You!

Stop Love Moralizing, Start Wising!

6. Love on Earth Must Be a Mentally Conquerable Force!

At the first stage of love growth, *the Love Risk Zone*, we all face the risk of falling for a wrong person or losing love due to the **LACK OF AWARENESS**. Love is occupying our thoughts from the very early years of life. We fantasize about love and **ROMANTICIZE it,** making up a fairy tale of a tormenting expectation of love. Unfortunately, the reality proves that we build up wrong schemes in the mind and expect them to be realized according to our expectations.

But *love skills* need to be developed on the basis of the engraved in us *habits of love*. (See the Introduction) Love habits and skills are forming together the unity of the **FORM + CONTENT** of love that is generating the *personal integrity* of a man / woman on the track of Self-Resurrection.

Form + Content

(Body+ Spirit+ Mind) + (Self-Consciousness + Universal Consciousness) = *The Whole Self!*

The form and content of love are being developed by the universal paradigm:

Synthesis – Analysis - Synthesis

The habits of love are planted in us from berth by our parents who instill them with their own love. The **LOVE HABITS** are also innate in us. They get developed gradually, **synthesizing** the best qualities of our parents and the mages of love that we see around. Next, the process of *analysis* starts that is always connected with the X-raying of an object of love. Finally, our emotions get *synthesized* again into beautiful **LOVE SKILLS.** that will never betray us if they were formed consciously and continuously.

Our Love Habits + Skills Form the Holistic Love Code Fields!

7. The Unconquerable Libido

Regrettably, our love relationships at present are governed by the **unconquered libido,** low values, and doubts about marriage being a limiting state of a person's free expression and self-realization.

Unconquered sexual energy generates love forgery!

When I write about the necessity to develop the **LOVE SKILLS** in our kids, I mean that we must teach them control their sexual energy as early as possible. The sacredness of love, instilled in the brain of a child will help him / her stay away from the uncontrolled impulses to masturbate that became a norm in this society. Such situation is generating men's early inevitable importance. The reservoir of the sexual energy gets depleted much earlier than it is supposed to happen.

Surprisingly, there are findings in science that even men's early baldness might relate to the inability to control their sexual energy and the lack of its expression in the true **HEART + MIND** love state. I think that a great deal of responsibility for the state of the unconquerable libido, ruling the body, be it a man or a woman, lies with a woman. No wonder, almost every proverb of King Solomon in the Bible, warns a man against " *a strange woman."*

"My son, if a strange woman entices thee, consent thou not!"

A woman should never stop being a mother, a lover, a caretaker, and a friend. The conquered libido will return us to the state of respect for men – *the generators of life that women are supposed to create and nurture.* Our society has lost this respect, and therefore, women do not enjoy full reverence, either. We need to learn to commit to the deeds of love, without expecting" *What's in it for me?"* stuff! Without doubt, the channels of love perception must be clean, and **the** *well-developed love skills* will help our kids empower their libido consciously. As a result, they will be much happier in their love life later, keeping the love libido under the control of the mind's store!

Less is More!

8. Sexual Re-Lay is at Play!

I think that we are living at present in the **"Kingdom of Crooked Mirrors."** The US President is marred in public, men are humiliated, disrespected, and under-loved. Women tend to call men "jerks," blaming them for the sex advances that had occurred years before. Both sexes appear to be altogether inconsiderate of the ethical impact of such behavior on kids.

Besides, women are becoming more and more *materialistic, demanding, morally unstable, and constantly discontent.* Their incessive demands ruin the very spirit of love relationships that often turns into *a manipulative game*. Women then blame men for having preferred the company of more considerate males. The reverse picture is actual, too, in the female love domain.

" *Love is a free agent."* (*Delia Lama*)

The lack of **MORAL MATURITY** in both sexes is appalling now. It's noteworthy that parents all over the world cherish the name of the school their kids will graduate from much more than the quality of education they will acquire and the people that they will become. We do not process a personality growth on the ladder of life *physically, emotionally, mentally, spiritually and universally!* The concern for how much money young people will make after college graduation outshines the level of **INTELLIGENCE** and **MORAL INTEGRITY.**

<u>*"Don't teach just the subject. Teach the whole person!*</u>"(*Leo Vygotsky*)

It's obvious now that the best, truly intelligent students *from the Ivy league schools* may be far from being the best in their inner qualities. The title of the school students graduate from does not reflect *the personable values of the graduates.* Frank Broony rightfully notes,

"The school you enter does not define who you will become."

Apparently, we do not teach our young generation, living their technologically enhanced lives, to value the essential standpoints of ethics and morality. Time demands that their education be focused on building up personalities in an inseparable link of **MIND+ HEART** connection. Then, bulling and sexual orientation surprises will become less painful. Our respect for each other will be based on **the *conceptual structure*** of the new living and loving.

"No seed grows without support." *(Proverb 19),*

I am also certain that ***sexual orientation*** is a personal business that should not be discussed in public, ruining someone's self-confidence, a political career, and a family life. ***We should better fertilize our life with drops of kindness and consideration, not sex frustration!***

We are governed by the Universal Laws of life that shape us irreversibly and make us answer the question who we love and why. ***The Law of Sow and Reap*** is to be observed as the fundamental one in love-ethics. *"Our thoughts are seeds, and the mind is the fertilized soil that produces the crops. Reap the drops of love from it"* (Edgar Cayce).

We inherit the values and traits of character from the parents, and we are supposed to be ***shaping our own personalities*** for the rest of our lives. Many great mothers and fathers have sacrificed the best time of their lives for the most noble mission of raising their kids, but the goal of their own self-realization is often not accomplished.

It's not right! It's never too late to choose the Self- Salvation fate!

Finally, *the Law of Sow and Reap* is directly connected ***to the auto-inductive work*** that we all need to do continuously, helping to program our cells against evil life spells. Every chapter in this book ends with a self-induction of ***an inspirational, mind-sowing character*** that generalizes the concept of the chapter and backs up the spirit of self-transformation and love elation. Use them.

Strengthen your Personal Gene with the Self-Suggestive Hygiene!

9. *Love is the Freedom of Choice and Your Personal Voice!*

Love in its every form should not be blurred or marred by mass media or the society's indoctrination. *Life is the quality of your self-consciousness,* not sexual orientation, or the number of years on your personal calendar. Regrettably, what we witness now is the distortion of love in its social understanding, twisted by the mass media's declaration of some one's sexual orientation, and, therefore, a dirty perception of gay love in the minds of the general public. Love doesn't have national, racial, religious, or gender limitations!

"The world is the Thinking God, and love is our free symbol of the unity with God." (Joseph Murphy)

As free beings, we have a free will to decide who to love and how. As long as love remains the main stimulus for a person's **SELF-RESURRECTION**, no one has the right to interfere with anyone's personal growth. Naturally, declaring one's sexual orientation in public and mass media's reviewing the dirty details of some one's sexual seduction are ethically unacceptable, *It's not our business!*

Even though I do not support any religious warnings about committing a sin for a wrongdoing, such behavior does constitute a sin, and it will be punished from the Above. *Somerset Maugham*, in his great novel " *The Moon and Sixpence*" reminds us of the boomerang in this respect,

" The mills of God grind slowly, but they grind exceedingly small."

To enlighten our consciousness and raise the self-consciousness of our kids, we should not make anyone's sexual orientation public, thus planting a wrong idea in the young, unformed minds that now openly declare their alleged sexuality "as cool." They need ethical knowledge, to be able to respect a personal **LOVE RIGHT**. Also, considering the transgenders' rights as those of women in sport is ridiculous, too. Men are energetically enhanced differently, and their physical aptitudes are naturally overwhelmingly higher.

Love is the Link of the Mind and the Heart, not just the Genitals at that!

10. Marriage is the Bond of Responsibility and Love Reward!

Every Human Contact is a Responsibility!

"Why didn't you say you are my father?'- I am poorly made." (Steve Jobs)

"Love is an emotional river. In the conflict with your kids, get into the boat and cross it to their bank. Don't expect them to do it to you. They will cross it for their kids." *(A Russian proverb)*

The Parents' Tree of Love Security.

It Gets Reflected in the Kids' Soul's Purity!

11. The DNA of Love is Encoded in the Brain's Stuff!

I write above that *love needs spiritual maturity*, and it grows together with a young man or a young girl from a very early age, forming the **LOVE GRAVITATIONAL BASIS** for life. Boys view love as a very sacred phenomenon at the start of their self-identification. Girls are expecting love to come from everywhere, and they visualize their wedding ceremonies and motherhood from a very early age.

The sacredness of a parenthood is under the mind's hood!

Expectations and demands are encoded in a woman's DNA. A woman in love, like a spider, is weaving its net of a family in her mind, and she places the man in the center of her love web. becoming very watchful and possessive for the web not to be ever broken by any intruder. Naturally, *a man becomes encoded in her DNA* because a woman is *love centered. Somerset Maugham* noted rightfully,

"Women can think about love all day long; men - only at times."

A woman's mission is love production, and it is based on the **LOVE SKILLS** that get transformed into **HEART + MIND** unity and develop naturally with marriage and the birth of kids A man's DNA is not weaved around the family, and a woman never changes it unless a man transcends his original creative role and gains a woman's love qualities. His role is to evolutionary change the world!

A man is love de-centralized and less heart- wise!

A man's love web is structured around his job, his creative mission on earth, his protective role in life. A woman does not get structured into his DNA because men are *love decentered*. A man, being heterogenic in his physical nature, is meant to catch a lot of victims of love into his love web. Naturally, many brainless flies get stuck in his web now and then, and he can hardly do anything about it. That is a man's mission in love production, and it is based on the **LOVE HABITS,** encoded in his DNA and not formed with *the mind+ heart unity* that can be instilled in him by a loving, considerate mother, or a wise woman later.

Habits + Skills make up the joint love fields!

The connection of the habits and skills or *the form + content of love* build up a long-term relationship that depends on the state of this link and is impossible without it. This connection explains why *women love with their hearts; men love with their minds.* According to the French people, men also love with their eyes, while women love with their ears. This wise observation is at the core of love *magnetization* and *de-magnetization.* Women get love-magnetized with compliments, flowers, and the words of admiration and love. *They need a verbal support of love.*

My dad, for instance, kept complimenting my mom every day even when she looked tired, dis-colored, and old. There were fresh flowers in their house every two weeks, and my mom always kept changing her outfits. My dad would interrupt any argument that mom might have started with him, saying out of the blue,

By the way, Ninochka, you look beautiful in this dress / blouse, etc."

When I asked him why he kept lying in this way while mom looked far from being beautiful, he would reply, *" I remember her young and beautiful, and this is how she will always be for me. Also, when I remind her of my love, she calms down, and we never have any ruinous fights."*

Obviously, men are very visual, and it is only natural they keep looking at beautiful women passing by. They are stimulated by beauty, great scents, *(called pheromones in biology),* and shapes. So, being casual about the looks, mindlessly dressed, and too demanding and talkative kills a man's sexual drive then and there, and women must blame themselves for being disregarded, neglected, or cheated on.

Love is in the Eye of the Beholder!

12. Simplify Your Life with Being More Alive!

(An Inspirational Booster)

Try to find beauty in ordinary things.

They are around us in strings!

The string theory of matter

Presents beauty in every gutter!

The beauty is everywhere;

It's in the ugly and fair!

So, adjust your vision

To seeing the invisible beauty provision

And unit it as One

With the universal Energy + Mind fun!

Thus, you'll make a leap

From potentiality to actuality

And unfold yourself in stride

To the Luminosity of life!

Invest into the greatest asset –Your Soul's Facet!

Enlightenment is being One with Thinking, Speaking, Feeling, and Seeing the Life's Fun!

13. Re-Invent Yourself in Every Cell!

A dynamic interplay of human consciousness that is changing rapidly with the technological evolution, demands every one's re-invention of Self, or **CONQUERING** of **SELF** in five levels: *physical, emotional, mental, spiritual, and universal holistically.*

The What + How + Why monitor the love drive!

It means that we should question our love attraction for *the physical, emotional, mental, spiritual, and universal reasons* behind it. Such **LOVE SCANNING** puts the mind and heart in synch and helps us obtain the **SYMMETRY** of the heart and mind that, according to *Dr. Steven Weinberg,* the Noble Prize winner, *"is underlying everything."*

More particularly, the holistic philosophy of self-development that I am outlining in every book on Self-Resurrection is meant to back you up in your self-installation by way of enhancing the growth of your self-consciousness in *a beautiful symmetry with the Universal Mind*. The individualized vision of life must come with full awareness of what life is all about in a new, technologically enhanced way.

We all have the gift of kindness and compassion at the bottom of our hearts, but we need to move these qualities to the forefront of our minds to be able to use them to our mutual advantage, de facto not just de juror. We must first *synthesize the form and the content* of the inner and outer lives in accord with the present moment to get more aware.. Next, we need *to analyze the life* we live by becoming more rational and self-consciousness driven.

Finally, we will establish connection with to the Universal Intelligence, make individualized conscious decisions and accomplish the right outcome in life, getting to *the final synthesis* of our well-lived or wasted lives. The holistic paradigm of life will become complete.

Synthesis - Analysis - Synthesis!

(For more, see in the previous books)

Visualize the Love Flight in Your Inner Sight!

(Pictures by Fred Cronin)

Love that's Flying is Never Dying!

14. Be a Self-Guru; Love is a Seasonal Phenomenon, too!

Neuroscience has it that the DNA, or our genetic material, reacts to our thinking, speaking, and feeling. The books we read, the music we listen to, and the subjects we discuss impact the wave genome, or the wave genetic program that is constantly changing from the negative to the positive. These programs are forming and re-forming us through *"reprogramming our cells." (Dr. Bruce Lipton)* In fact, our thoughts, words, and feelings are changing, transforming, and molding our reality. We know that water reflects, accepts, and preserves the programs that we communicate to it. The Sun is connected to our solar systems, made up by the electric circuit, formed by the unity of the heart and the mind, or by the **Merkabah.**" (*Drunvalo. Melchizedek)*).

Obviously, as a part of nature, we change inwardly with the change of seasons, too. The effect of **SYNCHRONIZATION** of our thinking and feeling with the Universal vibrations helps *us beat the stereotyped thinking and not-knowing*, and it makes us more perceptive of the changes in nature that we always respond to physically and emotionally. The Universal Field is the energy field that is creating harmony, and its spiritual system has a direct impact on us.

Our spiritual maturation is the effect of the synchronization!

. *In winter,* we accumulate wisdom and love. *In spring*, we experience the re-birth of self-worth. Therefore, many marriages happen in May, and the best love say is in May! *In summer,* our ideas ripen. We rest and refresh the fruition of our mission. *In Autumn*, we step forth in self-worth. We start a new school, a new business. We reflect on life, assess the family integrity, or we are ripping what we have sowed. It's the time of action for the brain function!

Let's Live in Sync with the Nature's Link!

15. Let's Regain the Sense of Shame!

In my childhood, the most favorite book of every boy and girl in the former Soviet Union was the book " *Adventures of Huckleberry Finn"* by Mark Twain. William Falkner wrote that Mark Twin was *"the first real American writer, and we are all his heirs since then."* Ernest Hemingway noted that *"all modern American literature originated from one book by Mark Twain-" Adventures of Huckleberry Finn."*

This book is a real study guide of ethics for our children that are carried away from the reality by the *"Harry Porter's* mystics now and that hardly ever read the book that teaches them to be responsive and responsible, respectful and loving – the values that once instilled in kids, never get betrayed by them as adults.

Unfortunately, we are losing ethical values, and *the lack of the sense of shame* is becoming a looming unethical menace. ***Everything goes! Sex sells! / Chase the dollar!*** These are the moral mottoes that are ruling our minds now. Our movies, TV shows, trashy books, and stand-out performances are overwhelmed with dirty scenes, rude profanity, naked body parts demonstrations, and general moral de-magnetization that is affecting our minds, hearts, and love rotting bodies. ***"The strongest and the most valuable virtue of a noble man is the Sense of Shame!"****(Confucius)*

In the novel " *Anna Karenina"* by a great Russian writer Leo Tolstoy - the classic about true love against social prejudices and restrictions, has a significant episode. After Anna openly confessed her affair with count Vronsky and her deep love for him to her husband, he tried to disregard this fact and claimed for his marital rights. Anna protested," *I can't. I am his wife now."* How many women / men can be that sincere now? *"Cheating pushes contradictions to their ultimate limit where one has to choose between madness and innocence. Simple free being becomes encrusted with the burdensome armor of the Ego."*

"Remorse is the Soul's Force!" *(Leo Tolstoy)*

16. Moral De-Magnetization is in Elation!

Many people now fight for *"the purity of their love"* and boldly protect it from public intrusion and spicy stories around it. The disconnection of the heart and the mind is a new norm that is killing our moral core, the essential love link of the *Merkabah* magnetic field.

The core of the Merkabah link is the body, the heart, and the mind in sync!

The sense of shame must be given back its boundaries installing status! Our kids should not consider showing the boobs, naked asses, throwing cakes in faces, and other nasty demonstrations of the lack of manners, accompanied with: *"Whatever; I don't care; What do I care?* to be normal and acceptable. Profanity also pollutes love, and it must be banned from the shows, movies, and other public programming means that pollute the sacredness of love streams.

Losing the sense of shame is not a fun game!

The evolution is pushing us to developing **THE UNIVERSAL CONSCIOUSNESS** and getting rid of the Americanized consciousness that is overpowering the globe now with its hungry chase for money and *moral de-magnetization*. The best qualities of the Americans are courtesy, generosity, and creative magnetism.

The USA is the country of great values and ideas, of the leading science and technology, great minds and spiritually inspiring hearts. The American input into the world's civilization cannot be underestimated, I hope that this country will regain its *status of the moral and spiritual leader* too. The best of us can forestall the wave of dirty immorality and grow personality-wise, like it has never been dreamed of in any other country of the world thanks to the country's potential goodness.

<u>*May the global chaos and crisis stop ruining our love devices!*</u>

Let's Not Repose at cleaning the Body's Foes and the Mind's Moles!

17. Hasty Loving Ends in Whining!

One of the symptoms of **"the Cupid complex "by Dr. Pearsall** that I have commented on above, is a muddled, unaware, hasty loving when a person thinks that he is in love or he is love-struck and crazy about someone, while he / she knows nothing about the object of his / her admiration. **Such relationship cannot get love- charged** because it is blind with romantic expectations, enticed by the imitated movie scenes of hasty undressing of each other and falling into a bed, not into a real love. Self-demagnetization of the person's **MERKABAH** is always the consequence of such " *hasty loving.*"

Irrationality is the reason for quick-fix relationships that deplete the soul and turn it into a self-guilt mole.

Love is not happening. It is a growing, on-going, and out-going process of commitment and re-commitment, investment and re-investment in five levels of our *holistic self-growth - physical, emotional, mental, spiritual, and universal.* It needs to mature with the *spiritual* sharing and *intellectual* identifying of each other, in a tactful consideration of the person's *emotional* buttons, and finally, love culminates in the *physical* attraction, magnetized by the mind-monitoring and lasting passion.

To be consciously love -content means to be self-confident!

Also, in a love relationship, don't say and do what you will regret later. It is always true that it's more hurtful to feel regrets that you didn't say and do something at the right time, than control yourself in time and space. This is when praying comes to help. <u>**Praying should be a sincere process of self-X-raying, self-forgiving, and self-reforming.**</u> Praying is also a creative process that should always start with the expression of gratitude, processing the conscience through self-analysis, and concluding it with reasoning out the missteps.

Conscience is Our Direct Line with Stay Aboard!

Inner Love Ugliness destroys Your Loveliness!

"Bad habits have a good tendency – Either you kill them, or they kill you!"

(Albert Einstein)

18. The Gift of Love Must Be Instilled by the Returned Love!

We must admit that intelligence, wisdom and sensitivity are our best virtues, and the ability to love and to fill up our kids' hearts and minds with the sense of beauty is our primary concern.

We reap what we sow!

It's time we realized that criticizing and rejecting, *using hurtful sarcasm and constant fun-making are soul-breaking!* I don't think it is a character-building and love-enhancing encouragement to tell a child, heading to school, "*Have fun!*" and ask him / her when they are back from school, "*Did you have fun?*" Why don't we remember great maxima by **Ecclesiastes** that teaches the humanity to value time and urges us to use it consciously for centuries on end.

"A time to plant and a time to pluck up that which is planted."

Our mothers and the loved ones, the first love, a respected woman at work, a sincere friend, an author, a psychiatrist, a woman of wisdom, and the Mother Nature together form our mentality and shape our souls. But when women serve their love wholeheartedly and devotedly, they are not servants. *They are the sculptors of their men's souls!*

Love and intelligence must be defined by love diligence!

The hearts of mothers and the minds of men are forming our Love Stem! Hurray to all of them! So, women, please, respect men – *the creators of the outside life around you!* And men, please, respect women – *the creators of the inside of you!* Being suspicious and mistrusting is a common trend but listening to your own intuition will out-power any society-engraved doubt and fear. *Trust and respect yourself to trust and respect others*! Constantly induct yourself with:

Respect is Me;
Respect is My Philosophy!

19. Love Magnetism is Charged with Self-Reformism!

Love magnetism is directly connected with the inner balance, discipline, and order. The person whose emotions are in the turmoil of different flings and the chaos in the heart and the head can never be happy in love or make anyone happy. Don't be a temperamental guy. **Be a cool guy with a love-refined thigh!** The ability to love is, in fact, the ability to control your love *physically, emotionally, mentally, spiritually,* and *universally.*

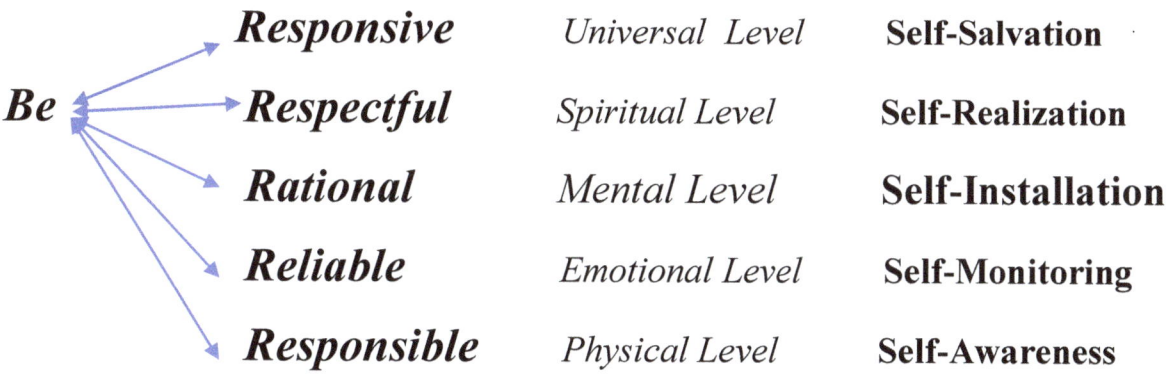

Be			
	Responsive	*Universal Level*	**Self-Salvation**
	Respectful	*Spiritual Level*	**Self-Realization**
	Rational	*Mental Level*	**Self-Installation**
	Reliable	*Emotional Level*	**Self-Monitoring**
	Responsible	*Physical Level*	**Self-Awareness**

Get into the habit of X-Raying your feelings holistically for their authenticity every day and give yourself a rational boost to energize your **MIND + HEART** link without any regrets or curses in sync. *With the sacred name of Jesus Christ, close your mouth to vice!*

Perfect your thoughts every day because they transform into feelings and actions. Test your thinking continuously and remember," *It takes only a stroke to change a minus into a plus!"* Scan your thoughts, feelings, and action for their positive charge, good intentions, and kindness. Your drops of kindness must be full of mindedness.

Praise yourself before going to bed for the good deeds done, whatever small they might be. Shake any psychological discomfort off your mind+ heart unity; preserve their purity! Remember the basic self-induction: for self-production must be:

I'm My Best Friend; I'm My Beginning and My End!

20. Love is Not Confusing; It's Soul Musing!

Finishing an overview of the **Risk Zone of Love**, allow me to remind you that we often sustain wrong relationships and marry wrong people. Many of us think that they don't deserve love, or that love is too confusing and treacherous. We don't take a risk to be deeply involved in a relationship for fear of being hurt or anchored. Men tend to resolve any problem through a quick sex, women - through impulsive shopping, house cleaning, making over, or a meaningless chatting with a friend or the best Internet suitor on a smart phone.

Killing time is killing Life!

Science has it that many men complain about feeling guilty after the sex since they do not want to obligate themselves in any way. The relationships that had seemingly blossomed on the physical level turn out to be either special or ordinary, and they normally end up in going to the next guy or a girl. Women, after years of waiting for their *Price Charming* and having "*kissed a hundred frogs*" turn out to be either **bitches or witches**, generating drama, or trying to resolve it in an evil, revengeful way. Men, after releasing the sexual tension in a quick fix relationship, feel empty in the mind and the heart. It happens because both men and women focus on wrong objectives in life **Read the 31 proverbs of King Solomon's wisdom in the Bible**, for every day of the month. They all teach us the wisdom of life and warn men not to waste it on "*strange women.*" Love comes to those who deserve it.

Self- Salvation is in Self-Realization!

It means that when we change our priorities from just ***physical*** improvement and sexual satisfaction to the realms of ***emotional*** diplomacy, ***mental*** enrichment, ***spiritual*** maturity, and the ***universal*** outlook, we expand the possibilities of a much happier life's nook.

Love is Not only a Feeling Thing; it's also a Thinking Thing!

21. The Inner Dignity of the Whole Forms the Aristocratism of the Soul!

Enlightenment is, in fact, *a holistic refinement of a person* that constitutes inner beauty and outshines any risks in love seeking. It's our overall wisdom that encompasses our *new, digitally backed up education,* demonstrating the necessity to sort it out in a new holistic way, applying it to our much better living and loving.

The Art of Loving is the Art of Learning!

As our self-awareness changes, *we start to live consciously*, with much more appreciation of life, expanding our love outlook with the new developments in science that change the thinking and perceiving mind. We are becoming more human, more rational, more aware of the consequences of our actions, and much stronger in the **PERSONAL GRAVITATIONAL POWER** that many of us have lost irreversibly. Personal gravity implies that we absolutely need to think not of the physical or mental improvement only. Our goal is holistic beautifying of life in five life dimensions.

We need to stop living on the automatic pilot of the mass-media governed riot!

Acquiring the *Living Intelligence holistically*, we are deepening our knowledge of the totality of life and *become aristocratic* in our souls. Also, we get better energized, more intellectualized, much better informed, and totally reformed! Finally, we start realizing the moral difference in ourselves because everything is perceived in comparison. *We start shining, illuminating our own life and the lives of others.* Obviously, there is no moral transformation without the mental one that presupposes that we become able to interpret God – the Universal Intelligence at work thanks to our rationally-emotionalized thinking.

A Holistic Me is an Aristocratic Me!

(End of the Love Zone One)

Harmony vs. Disharmony

(Pictures by Galina Morrel)

The Souls" Connection is in Love Reflection!

Love Zone Two

(Emotional Dimension)

Breach of Trust Zone

Expectation and Self-Justification

(The Self-Growth Level of Self – Monitoring)

Love Relation is Not a Completion; It's a Mission!

1. Illusion vs. Delusion

In its second phase, *the Breach of Trust Zone*, love is an emotional battlefield between illusion and delusion that are always mediated by confusion. When the exaltation of the first love is gone, we get disappointed and disillusioned. This is the most difficult period for the people in love because **the period of infatuation comes gradually to an end**. The time of hurtful episodes of misunderstanding, fights, and different perceptions of the reality is still turning into passionate make-ups, but love has a breach of doubts and hate sprouts. *"A man comes to the earth to conquer himself and the world. and to obtain the experience of the soul."(Edgar Cayce)*

Inner equilibrium is the hardest to instill in the cerebrum!

To create harmony in love, we need to acquire the love skills of a kind, compassionate, respectful, tolerant, and considerate person. Only then, can one create the space of love from the Above in his being.

"A happy man rarely goes to church. The suffering ones tend to frequent it". (Fyodor Dostoevsky)

It's always easier to be corrupt and ruined rather than decent and ethical. The states of love are always weighed down by hatred, indifference, and anger-the states that generate disharmony, disbalance, and self-destruction. Check the Love Code above. (*Part Three*)

<u>Instill Your Own Love Code in the brain and be overly sane!</u>

A woman with her center- directed attitude to love generates *an off-the-center attitude* in a man. Therefore, the saying *"Give me some space"* is more meaningful for a man, and if a woman has respect for his ambitions and stands behind him, the union of their hearts and minds will magnetize their relationship, or marriage for years. But if the heart is disconnected with the mind, a person lives in disharmony and *constant search for a soul mate*. How can a lost heart become whole if there is no conscious and consistent programming from the mind?

Every Heart needs to Be Schooled!

2. Any Soul's Recovery is in Love's Discovery!

I keep accentuating the point that *Self-Actualization of the mind should go in line with the love formation in the heart*. As a matter of fact, love from the Above does not reside in the heart of a man / woman that has no self-esteem in the mind.

Self-esteem is the mind + heart's joint stream!

We are often very much absorbed by *the routine of an empty life to the brim.* No wonder, we feel unhappy after numerous flops of love. Many people consider themselves to be god forsaken, lost, disgraced, betrayed, and double crossed in the relationships that qualify them as losers in life and love. To find a loyal partner in life, you need to be someone with the **SPINE OF LOVE** yourself. Love is wrecked by the routine thinking, speaking, feeling, and loving!

That's why love is starving!

It's vital to develop good habits of making the bed, cleaning the teeth, putting things in order, being neat, respectful and polite, etc., but it's also paramount to discriminate routine good habits from *the stereotyped behavior habits* that ruin the enthusiasm of having change and making different choices in life and love. Again,

The choices we make, dictate the live we live!

Many relationships and families are destroyed by the stereotyped thinking of women who obligate their men with never ending " *You should...)* Routine expectations, demands, house rules, and casual love performances kill the very flavor of love between the love partners, parents and their kids, even between the pet owners and their pets. The spine of love is built on variety, sincerity, and honesty, as well as the consideration of a partner's mood. The way we don't like to eat the same food day in and day out, *our minds and hearts hate routine and stereotyping of our perception of love and life.*

Love, Marry, and Make Love Only for Love!

3. The Harmony of Love is a Very Fragile Stuff!

Our reception of the avalanche of the information that we are getting on our smart phones must be sifted for its validity for our intelligence expansion and self-growth. The stereotyped way, prompted by the mass media programs our cells in the most harmful and routine way.

If we don't resist, we get into the vortex of the commonsense mist!

People live and love, imitating the episodes in the movies, quickly undressing the partner, throwing cakes in faces, using the humiliating phrases and curses etc. Such behavior demonstrates disrespect for their *love spine and the* **LOVE CODE** that every couple should work out for themselves.

The Love Code's laws might be occasionally broken but the loved one is not prosecuted till the final sentence is announced. *Forgiveness is the virtue of love re-filling and re-living!* Always give your love a second, third, fourth, fifth etc. chance Don't be love impulsive, vindictive, and divisive! Love needs to be nurtured and supported, but not *physically, emotionally, mentally, spiritually, and universally distorted* Process it every night through a quick assessment test and let it always be abreast! The words "**I Love You**" must be your philosophical guru, and the unity of a man's mind and a woman's heart your second half! Make your love the authentic life gulf!

"The first marriage is granted by God;

The second one is from the people;

The third one is from the devil!"

(The Russian folk wisdom)

May Your Love Elation Never Know Love Frustration!

4. Love or Lust; Who Can I Trust?

(An Inspirational Booster)

I coax my daughter, as all moms do,
To end her endless love ado,
"To turn love into a marital bliss"
Love the one you are with!"
Mom, she retorts,
Breaking the train of my thoughts,
"There is no love; it's only lust
That takes the grips on us so fast!
When you are in the USA
It's a one-night stand that has its say!"
Therefore, it's hard to tell today
Which is love or lust, per say
The evils of a one-night stand
Ruin the love castle sand
Love goes down the drain
In our instant gratification brain!
The hopes and stomach butterflies
Have the life span of daily flies!
Marriage lasts, but a little while
It even stars with a sarcastic devilish smile!
It's the money force
That rules any love's worth!

Being loaded

Is what makes love molded!

Without a solid financial stand

You've got love with no refund!

The cancer of such love value

Spreads worldwide with the speed of the mildew.

Is there any review on how to turn love mildew

Into the pure love-lasting dew

That reflects the sunrise of passion

And the sunset of compassion,

That has much understanding

And demonstrates no mutual respect withstanding!

We need love that forms

Inspires and transforms!

But such love needs to be taught and learnt;

It must be reinstalled in our young generation's Fort!

And since love in everyone's gene,

It should also be released on the social scene!

The Love of God is the What We Reflect in Every Action and Each Thought!

5. Love Pollution has become Our Common Social Constitution!

Love has a freedom of choice, and no one has the right to get inside its closed doors. But the society needs to restore <u>**the form and the content**</u> of a personal expression of love that is an evolutionary process. It cannot be pushed, stigmatized, **DIRTILY DEMOCRATIZED**.

The definition of intolerance is too extended in this respect now.

The evil is not a person's sexual orientation.

It's an individual's choice, and everyone has his /. her own reasons for it. Evil is in the way we demonstrate it and view it, polluting our own minds and hearts and those of our kids with dirty details and blind judgements. Consequently, we are killing the seed of love in its universal sense.

Don't be love-snappy! Make Someone Happy!

I see gay parades and " *going out of the closet*" as an expression of the right to protect love from its dirty interpretation and an open unfair segregation. Who are the judges? Don't we generate the distortion of love with our scorn and the mass media narrow-mindedness stuff?

Let love be, and let's not pollute its social sea!

Love pollution is not in a sexual orientation It's in the way we see it, deleting the very concept of love from the society with our dirty treatment of a very individual choice, thus, distorting the beauty of a human relationship to the point when tolerance turns into *a tactless intolerance* that has turned the gay movement into a trend..

To stay together, the two love webs need to be enclosed into the third web, created by God,

We should not interfere with *the Universal Intelligence Web* that brings us together. to begin with. This web is much stronger magnetically because it is weaved by the ethical values, beliefs, and the spirt of self-formation. Rabbi P. S. Berg, the author of a very wisdom-generating book *"Taming the Chaos,"* writes that we can tame *the three beasts* that get us into the disbalance (**MIND+ HEART+ SEX**) only if we put them under the control of the conscious mind. Rabbi Berg's Kabalistic philosophy calls on us to establish **THE ORDER** in life and reverse the life from the disbalance of **666** *(the symbol of death)* to **999** *(the symbol of life)*.

To be One of the Love Cells - Tame Yourselves!

(For more, See the book *"Self-Taming!"* -Spiritual dimension)

Love is the emotion of intelligence because intelligence is life itself!

You can change your brain only in unity with the heart. How you think and how you feel create your state of being. So, ***you need to recondition the body for a new mind***, and do it in the auto-suggestive, or self-hypnotizing way.

We need to tame the body like we tame an animal!

We can change the brain only in unity with the heart. It's like planting the seeds of intelligence into the barren, rocky soil. Unfortunately, there is *a tendency now to redirect the Universal Love Flow* and let the mind respond to the body.

Such situation generates a completely distorted perception of life and its generator – love.

The hormones display becomes more meaningful and valuable than intelligence. I think that the love-emancipated position of a woman is responsible for the appearance of many deviations from the regular *"stream of consciousness technique."*

We need to be overly blunt on the love destroying front!

Don't Over-Ride the Love Site with Your Sex Might!

7. Moral Intelligence and Love Magnetism without Racism and Sexism!

More self-awareness means more wholeness, and therefore, *more quality of life!* An intelligent person constitutes the unity of the most important aspects of intelligence in lieu with the cosmic laws of which *the Law of Sow and Reap* is the first one to consider. When you live in the awareness of this law, the best human features translate into human integrity, devoid of any prejudices of racism, chauvinism, or sexism. *To be stable, love doesn't need any label!*

"To harvest good fruit, cultivate good thought about yourself." (Buddha)

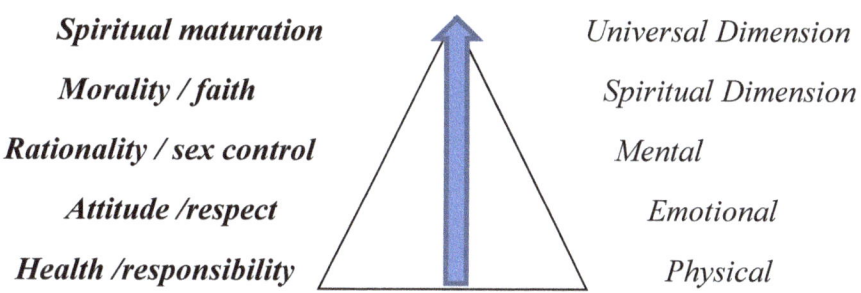

A bad person is living under the evil effect of progressive de-magnetization and de-humanization that ruin his *Informational Field* and eventually himself.

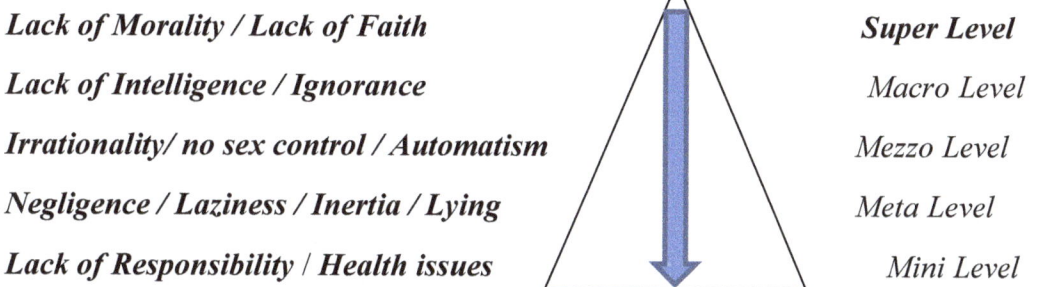

To stop the downfall of a personality development is not altogether impossible, *but it requires a lot of intelligence, self-monitoring and self-control.* As I have indicated above, self-monitoring in love cultivates inner balance of morality and personal integrity. The present-day science tries to get to the bottom of *the concept of impulsivity* that breaks us in half and pushes us away from the balance in love.

Love by the Moral Code; Love is in Our Spiritual Mold!

Live in God's Standards, Not in Crowd's Grandeurs!

The Love that was Betrayed has No time Rebate!

"Hate eventually subsides, offence gets forgotten with time, range cools down, but disappointment with the person who betrayed you never leaves."

(Fyodor Dostoevsky)

"All the Hearts are Unlocked with One Key – Love." (King Solomon)

8. Love Intelligence is Hard to Obtain and Regain!

LOVE INTELLIGENCE is the hardest intelligence to obtain of all! We must be trained for it from the earliest age possible. It is never too early or too late to **CHANGE YOUR LOVE FATE!**

Intuition is the language of the soul. Listen to it not to love retreat!

The philosophy of love hasn't been absorbed by our *minds and hearts in sync* for centuries because we were ignorant about it. But now Neuroscience has proved that love is" *hardwired into the architecture of our brains, not hearts."* We can conclude that a self-quest that starts with self-love is meaningless unless it is inspired by love for life and the people that inhabit it All the world masterpieces, the greatest innovations in science, the best pieces of art, literature, music, and poetry were created under the most inspiring emotion of love. The more love we radiate in the unity of its content and form, **the cleaner conscience** we have in return. Here's a joke by *Faina Ranevskaya,*

" *Everyone has conscience, but they do not carry it along all the time for fear to lose it."*

The present-day market is competing for such holistically developed, conscientious people. Quoting a wonderful book "*Taming the Chaos*" by Rev. Berg again, we need *to focus our love intelligence* and the willpower on governing the three main aspects of *"human's reformation of a soul – the mind, the heart, and the sex."*

Mind+ Heart + Sex must be a consciously- controlled process!

These are the three beasts that we need to tame because "*they make up the sacred unity of **999** and destroy the evil **666 links** of the fundamental forces of life"* (Rev. Berg). that constitute order and chaos, evolution and entropy, construction and destruction.

Our Main Life Action is the Holistic Self-Construction!

9. The Authentic Love from the Above is Becoming Viral Now. Wow!

More and more people at present realize the need for enlightenment of their family life and relationships. The leading role in this process is with women that are the heart of the relationship the **GRAVITATIONAL FORCE** of it.

The United States is *the country of Self-Realization and a woman's creative emancipation.* It is the main incentive for an immigration. This country builds you up personality-wise, and it opens the horizons of opportunities that are very challenging and overwhelmingly hard for *Self-Installation* in life both men and women but are still possible if the person learns to love a new home and give the best he / she has for it..

The authenticity of self is in the love cell!

Thousands of immigrants from all over the world of both sexes could accomplish success that might have been unthinkable in their own countries.

The outburst of creativity in people thanks to the technological expansion of thought is mind-blowing, but the heart's development is slowing!

The self-formation changes are technologically and personally viral, but they must be beyond survival, freeing both men and women from the routine cores and distractions, killing the love spark and deviating from the path of Self-Resurrection

That's must be our next great evolutionary accomplishment!

Reasoning psychologically, we must admit that both women and men consider themselves to be seriously under-loved and under-appreciated. That appears to be one of the reasons for sexual re-orientation in love formation.

But if we prioritize self-actualization and self-realization in life from an early age, we'll manage to change ourselves consciously, and we'll enjoy the consciously controlled consequences!

You'll both live and love and that's the new life stuff!

The role of a man as the mind and a woman as the heart in a relationship of the two different or the same sexes will help us build a much healthier society, based on love. consideration, compassion and self-formation.

he perception of love as **the mind+ heart unity** will bind the two-loving people for years to come, and such relationship will stimulate the self-growth for both parties in the union.

Love is not complaining and whining;

Love is Shining!

I think that *Love Intelligence* and *Moral Intelligence* must be backed up by the society and whether we like it or not, there is no skipping this step on the ladder of evolution.

Then love pollution will be a solvable solution!

Let's Never Lose the Sight of Our Divine Might!

Respect Each Other's Space
with the Love Gravitating Grace!

You are Two Trees with Separate Trunk Nooks, but Love-Entangled Roots.

10. Piracy in Love Kills the Love Stuff!

(An Inspirational Booster)

Our ascension to the Love Olympus

Takes a lot of emotional surplus!

    It needs the shrewdness of a Venus

      To satisfy a man's love penis!

You must be a goddess to subdue

To the man's love rule in you!

    You also need to be ready to be a zombie for love,

    To serve, to care, and to repair, as a love dove!

Doves never fail one another,

They stick together, rather!

    Remember that a love dove in you

    Also needs to clean up the residue

Of your being quickly discontent in lieu

With being bored with love only for you two!

    Sorry, but a lovey-dovey life

    Means to try to survive

In a patient respect and care

That make us both beware

    That love can easily die

    Then and there!

Being obliged to stay together through thick and thin

Is, indeed, a very real thing!

Your piracy in love

Will never help love survive!

True love till the grave

Is very hard to save!

But the trust in love can be reserved

And tenderly preserved!

So, detox your talks,

And learn careful love walks!

If you want to be a love dove,

Respect the generated love stuff!

Like any law of the universe,

Love can never go in reverse!

But like everything in the cosmic fort

It can never be completely learnt!

Robbing Someone of Love is the Worst Sin Stuff!

(Self-Induction for Love Production)

Honesty is Me;

Honesty is My Love Philosophy!

11. If You Are Love-Lenient, Self-Demagnetization becomes Expedient!

Accumulation of positive energy or a positive charge in the heart is a gradual process, but *the love de-magnetization* occurs immediately when we act under the effect of an impulse, fear, anger, hate, jealousy, or envy. To protect yourself and your love from getting de-magnetized, you need to be conscious of your negative traits of character.

Change your mental, emotional, and physical code;

Mold yourself; mold!

We need to beat stereotyped thinking and not knowing. Being conscious means a great amount of self-awareness.

The love's fitness is the body's stillness!

But the stillness of the body and the mind is being disturbed now by an avalanche of lies, stretching of the truth, playing love games, and manipulating with sex. *Lying and unforgiveness weigh as a heavy burden on the soul.* These spiritual inadequacies are the indication of the **INNER SLAVERY** to the hurting memories, engraved in the sub-conscious mind. They block your thinking and feeling and cause the de-magnetization of your Merkabah. They generate *the breach in the heart + mind unity*. So, the Know-How of its healing is yours!

We live in the pretty shallow time, but let's not whine!

You need to dig down deep to reach the sense of **AUTHENTICITY AND SINCERITY** that a new generation has lost and that are very difficult to be attained once the soul gets de-magnetized. Start paying aware attention to your thoughts and feelings. Get busy with discovering the reasons for lack of personal magnetism *Make a functionable solutions to be honest to yourself in your inner sell.* Help the actionable decisions about your self-growth become the fundamentals of your life at home, at work, and in all relationships with people. Be very picky who you chose to be around with.

Self-Refining is Living without Love-Manipulation and Lying!

12. Sex Without Love is a Bluff!

(An Inspirational Booster)

I coax my daughter, as all mom's do,

To end her endless love ado,

    "To turn love into a marital bliss"

    Love the one you are with!"

Mom, she retorts,

Breaking the train of my thoughts,

    "There is no love; it's only lust

    That takes the grips on us so fast!

When you are in the USA

It's a one-night stand that has its say!"

    Therefore, it's hard to tell today

    Which is love or lust, per say

The evils of a one-night stand

Ruin the love castle sand

    Love goes down the drain

    In our instant gratification brain!

The hopes and stomach butterflies

Have the life span of daily flies!

    Marriage lasts, but a little while

    It even stars with a sarcastic devil's smile!

It's the money force

That rules any love's worth!

Being loaded

Is what makes love molded!

Without a solid financial stand

You've got love with no refund!

The cancer of such love value

Spreads worldwide with the speed of the mildew

Is there any review on how to turn love mildew

Into pure love-lasting dew

That reflects the sunrise of passion

And the sunset of compassion,

That has much understanding

And is no mutual respect withstanding!

We need love that forms

Inspires and transforms!

But such love needs to be taught and learnt;

It must be reinstalled in our young generation's Fort!

And since it's in everyone's gene,

It should also be released on the social scene!

Only Aware Attention Stops Love Retention!

So, Love by the Moral Code;

Love is in Our Spiritual Mold!

13. Do Love Induction for a Better Love Function!

Self-assessment and self-reflection are the indispensable tools in the evolution of a human soul, constructed on love for oneself and others. That's why aware attention must be paid to the process of producing the outcome product - ***the holistic life and love awareness*** that are vital in raising self-consciousness. Rev. P. S. Berg writes,

Knowledge, based on awareness, is the origin of consciousness.

Here is a very simple **AUTO-SUGGESTIVE LOVE BOOST**. Apply it to yourself or your loved one. It works magically!

Rub the palms of your hands vigorously till they become very warm. Stand behind your loved one, put your hands on his / her shoulder so that the centers of your palms on both hands (the solar plexus area) lay on the edges of the shoulders of your loved one, on the rounding parts of both shoulders. **These are the spots of love perception!**

1). Start radiating love to his / her body from within, *calming him/ her down, and proving to yourself that love is the best empowerment of self and the other.* **2). Stand like that behind the person you love for a minute,** *till he /she feels calmed down and warmed up with the overwhelming feeling of your love for him / her.* **3) Start moving your hands slowly down his / her arms.** *When your hands come to the point where both palms meet, make a short pause and say,* **"I love you the way you are! 4). Finally, shake the hands off,** *as if removing any negative thoughts or feelings from his /her body and mind. Say out loud,*

"If any one doesn't love you, it's his or her problem, not mine!

Be sure to do the same for yourself, wrapping yourself up by the shoulders in a criss-cross manner. Feel the love for yourself. Change the induction accordingly.

The Core of Your Mer-Ka-Bah Link is the Heart and Mind's Sync!

14. Put the Strain on Your Sub-Conscious Brain!

Any soul's recovery

Is in the Merkabah's discovery!

      The mind's and the heart's link

        Must be in it in sync

With a person's soul

That can be self-consoled!

      The soul that is charged

        By the heart's surcharge;

The soul that resonates

To the rays of kindness, passion, and compassion!

      Then, the Sun's rays

        Will warm up the soul's space

Around a person's Merkabah

And delete his / her inner abracadabra!

      The sync of the heart's and the mind's harbor

        Will charge a personal Merkabah.

Your inner dissonance

Will give way to outer consonance,

      And you'll become One

        With the Everlasting Love under the Sun!

Emotional Chaos ruins the Mind's Heavens!

15. Motivate Your Love with Discipline and Consistency Stuff!

We need *to fight the pests of our love habits* - **LAZINESS AND LYING** every morning by motivating ourselves to be better with each new day. Try *launching yourself into a new day* by refreshing the love skills for yourself and the loved ones. Command to your spirit:

Tree -Two - One / or Five -Four-Three - Two -One! – START!

The one that is governed by acquiring **DISCIPLINE** and **LOVE SACREDNESS** in the unity of his / her heart and mind is always standing up for his / her *love uniqueness*. Therefore, true love is still surviving in *an avalanche of moral de-magnetization*: love fractions, filthy sex scenes, gay scandals, cheating, and numerous divorces

Take care of your internal pharmacy not to end up with love impotency!

Our love bank can be depleted of *the currency of love* because we have become too wasteful in this respect. *Every drop of kindness and consideration* should be viewed by us as our deposits into the love bank at every level of our self-growth and **SELF-RESURRECTION**
physically, emotionally, mentally, spiritually, and universally!
We enlighten ourselves and form solid love skills gradually but surely. Your being nice, compassionate, and sincerely considerate will help you beat impersonality and a casual attitude to love. We cannot love everyone, but *we can look at everyone with the loving eyes* and grant them with the drops of kindness if we can. The words " *Sweaty, Honey, Sugar, etc.* are commonly used, but they mean nothing if that are not backed up by love action. In a famous movie "*My Fair Lady,*" with a legendary *Audrey Hepburn,* Eliza sings repeatedly to her admirer's love declarations, *"You say you love me, prove it!"*

Love is not words; love is action without any love fraction!

Love Skills need a Lot of Love Refills!

16. The Next Step in Love-Defining is Living without Lying!

In my previous five books on *the Holistic Paradigm of Self-Creation*, I point out continuously that the first step on the path of self-formation or self-re-formation is to stop lying to yourself and others.

The hardest thing to do is to be authentically true!

It's so difficult to be honest because lying has become an addiction in our contemporary society. We keep lying to ourselves when we see that the person, we kind of like, is not exactly what he / she seems to be. Intuition is guiding us to a more thorough scanning, but we null these feelings and start justifying any of his / her faults, mis-speaking, or wrong-doings in the same fashion we do it to ourselves.

" Thoughts are the language of the brain; feelings are the language of the body" (Dr. Joe Dispenza)

We forcefully blind the realistic intuitive perception and *lull the voice of conscience* because we are not perfect ourselves. We compromise too much at the expense of *the inevitable soul-twisting and inner discomfort* that we try to hush down each time we face the situation in which a white lie seems justifiable or a serious twisting the truth appears to be absolutely unavoidable.

Double standards have become our guidance!

There are three enemies to fight on the path of love reformation. They are also *laziness, lack of enthusiasm, and lying!* These three ruinous love habits are driven by *the inertia of behavior,* engraved in the subconscious mind.

We can get rid of these pests with the help of **AWARE ATTENTION** switch that we need to be always ON to control constantly our thoughts and feelings.

Don't Be Rough, Be Love Tough!

17. A Family Life's Refining is in a Man's Role Redefining!

Love is a very controversial subject because its sanctity and sacredness have long drowned in sleezy jokes, unfaithful relationships, and a tough resistance to commitment of any sort.

No strings attached has become a regular love match!

Love has always been *a risk zone*, and people did make mistakes, trying to arrange and re-arrange their loves, retaining the freedom of the un-realized creative spirit at the same time. But *freedom needs the structure* to generate the energy of creation out of chaos.

The family pyramid must be topped by a man!

A famous Georgian proverb says, **"Happiness is a good man in the house!"** I agree with this statement, and I am confident that we should **give a man his leading role on a family track back.** A man is the priority force in creation, and we should not take this role from him." *First comes the energy than the matter. Matter is an infinite expression of the forms of light, and energy is much older than matter."(Nikola Tesla)*

A man is the mental energy of creation!

The heartbeat is the expression of the symphony of the Earth, and women are responsible for its harmonious music because they *orchestrate this rhythm in the hearts and minds of men and their children.* Love is a risky life seat ; Risk it!

Join your hearts and mind and grow together in life twines!

The rewarding feeling of belonging and root connection is worth the waste inflexion. Direct your family ship and steer it together through the roughest waters in life. ***Your heart + mind united life will thrive!***

The Family's Link is a Man's Mind + a Woman's Heart in Sync!

Be Self Love Governable,

Not Mass Media Programmable!

18. What Women Want for a Love Reward

The question in the title of this chunk of information is the one that even such love guru as *Sigmund Fraud* couldn't answer, and it still bothers every man. **So, what do women want?** A great American actor, *Mel Gibson* together with a very insightful actress *Helen Hunt* try to answer this question in the movie with the same title. However, the answer to this question is so multi-dimensional that even their excellent work has just revealed a few layers. Below, there is a small tale that might help us see the question *from the new times love angle.*

Once upon a time, the capital city of **King Arthur** *was surrounded by the enemy army, The leader of that army sent King Arthur a letter in which he put the condition that he would remove the siege of the city if King Arthur answered one very serious question to him within three days.*

The question was: **What do women really want?**

*King Arthur has asked every woman in the kingdom for the answer to this question, but none of them gave him the answer. Finally, he was informed that an old, ugly-looking which was ready to give him a straight-forward answer, but the prize would be very high. The king had no choice, and he asked the old which what the price was. The which wanted to be married to the best knight in the kingdom and the best friend of the king—***Haven*** by name. The which was so horrible-looking, angry and bad-mannered that King Arthur refused point blank to make his friend the victim of this condition.*

However, he told his friend about it, and surprisingly, Haven agreed to meet this condition for the sake of the freedom of his people. After that, the which answered King Arthur's question. She said,

"More than anything in the world, women want to master their lives themselves!"

After that, the siege was taken off, everyone was rejoicing, and the time of Haven's wedding came. When the time for the wedding night arrived, Haven, feeling very uncomfortable and disgusted e, entered the boudoir. Great was his surprise when instead of an ugly which, he saw the woman of a great beauty, lying in his bed. Haven asked her what had happened.

The which explained that in response for his kindness to her, she was ready to share her time with him as a very beautiful woman and an ugly old bitch. Then, she added that **he had to chose what kind of woman he wanted her to be** *during the day and what kind of woman he would like to have at night.*

Haven began to ponder on this choice. Would he rather be seen with a beautiful woman during the day and spend the night with an ugly witch, or should he spend the day with an angry bitch but go to bed with a desirable woman. Finally, **Haven decided to ask his wife to make the choice herself.**

After the witch heard his decision, she said that from then on, she would always be a beauty because he respected her opinion and gave her the chance to master her life herself!

_You cannot cage love; Love is a free stuff!

Don't live in a sad glue,

Don't regret the past dew,

Don't guess what's there to come,

Take care of today's outcome!

The Choices We Make dictate the Life we Live!

19. Emotional Control is Our Love Gravitational Goal!

Love has essentially an emotional basis, but we need to make it *mentally emotional* because, according to the neuroscientists, love is not located in the heart, it's in the mind. In any nerve-breaking situation, we need to immediately restore the *mind+ heart connection.*

Love has a neurological basis; it's a mentally emotional oasis!

Love hurts and emotionally makes you distraught if you haven't mastered the skill to ground your *physical, emotional, mental, and spiritual* pains holistically, consciously, and consistently. If you get into the habit of processing your thoughts, words, feelings and actions through *the matrix of self-assessment in each level*, your center of **SELF-GRAVITY** will be formed. You will stop being the victim of your past and the slave of the bad habits that" *have a good tendency – either you kill them, or they kill you". (Albert Einstein)*

Learn to ground your emotional un-rest with

Self- Assessment tests!

Being consciously aware of the reality activates the neuron connections in the brain that had been established previously with knowledge and self-control. Good, consciously controlled **LOVE SKILLS** get harbored in your memory bank. They become active the moment your *inner grace grants them the aware attention of love connection*. Your **LOVE GRAVITY** that had become stronger magnetically in the course of your relationship or marriage for years will help you gain the inner peace and the love sanity back. The emotional impulsivity will subside, and you will be yourself again, able to help the other party calm down. Being calm beats the nervous scum!

Love is the Best Teacher of Life,
It grounds You in the Life's Stride!

20. The Method of Substitution is the Solution!

The words of Albert Einstein above are a great illustration of the harmful role of had habits that we have harbored in the sub-conscious mind for years. Negative thinking is not the worst of them. We know also that our words affect the DNA and health in the most harmful way. Being talkative, feeling pity for oneself, exaggerating the consequences of your wrong actions, sharing with the people whose spiritual vibrations are lower than yours must be resisted! Again,

To self-redefine, be none with second standards, laziness, and lying!

Psychology calls this method – the **STATE OF SUBSTITUTION** when *"thinking about white monkeys"* should be substituted by *"thinking about pink elephants."* Obviously, *the shift of aware attention* from the object of trouble helps remove this troublemaker from the screen of your attention and substitute it with a much less bothering one. Yelling, cursing, sharing with wrong people, re-living the traumatizing scenario of the past, thinking about what *you should've, could've, would've* said or done damages your cells. Our cells and the entire genetic material are not indifferent to the sounds we hear, the thoughts we generate, the feelings we have, and the words we say. Everything in the bodily machine is interconnected and inter-reflected! So, park it calmly at a beautiful space of faith!

Relax and rest! Have the loving meditation fest! (See Above)

Also, don't be in a hurry to call someone, and if you did do it by force of habit, talk about the problem that bothers your friend to help him / her calm down, too. Thus, you'll be *switching your attention to a mental / emotional substitute.* Look around and perceive the beauty and the order of the nature as opposed to the chaotic life around.

Self-Sufficiency and Self-Reliance Mustn't be in Defiance!

Are You a Nervous Person?

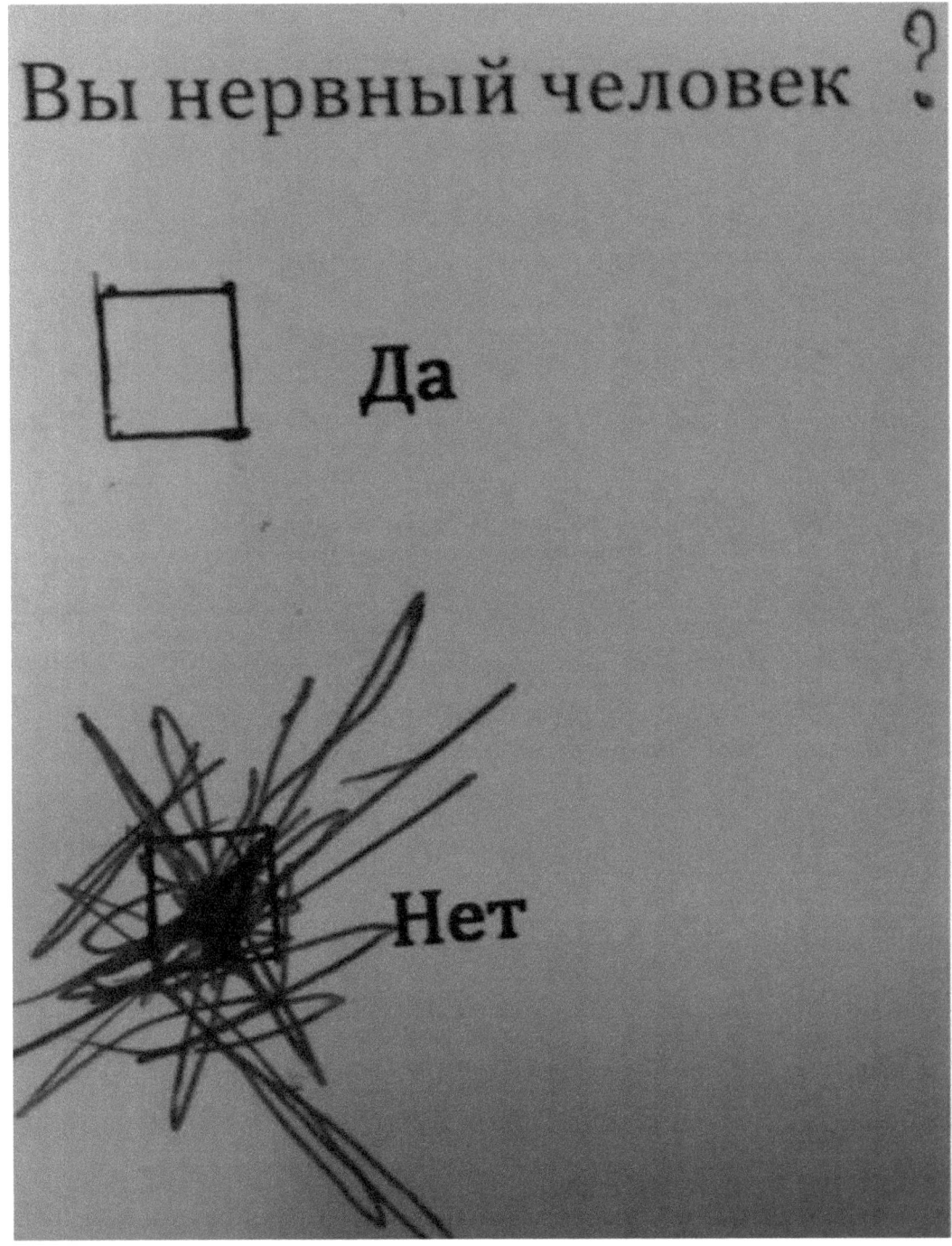

Yes or No.
Which Way do You Go?

21. Active Meditation on the Love Beach of the Self-Reflection Switch.

1. Lie flat on the back on the floor. Close your eyes and focus your aware attention on different parts of the body, switching your attention from the top of the head to the toes in a slow, respectful fashion. You are Godly in the Godless World! **Balance is your reward!**

*2. Fill the part of the body of your own choice or health necessity with the Sun light. Feel consciousness and life energy in it **for 15 seconds** and embrace it with love. **You are on the love beach. Enjoy the sun rays' switch!***

3. Let your aware attention run through the body like the Sun rays do when you are lying in its embracing light on the beach. **Let the Sun light run through your entire body** *a few times from head to feet and from feet to the head. Inwardly, induct yourself with breathing in the first part of the induction and breathing out the second one.*

I am one of the Sun's rays ; the Sun is in my time and my space!

4. Feel the body as a single, whole field of energy, **as One with the Unified Field of Energy** *in the Universe.*

I am One / with everything under the Sun!

5. Finally, breathe in light and love, and breathe out darkness and weakness. Flood your body with Higher Consciousness in the morning and before going to bed. Let your being be consciously energy fed!. Finish the meditation with the inductions at the bottom.

Light in, darkness out! Health in, sickness out!

Love in, hate out! *etc.*

Life is Going On, and it's Great to Have Been Born!

22. The Unity of the Hearts and Minds Binds!

Many inspirational talks on You Tube have appeared lately, presented by many great actors who teach us how to live more constructed lives. Their psyche has been professionally trained to play the roles of very good people and the villains. Changing the *physical, emotional, mental, spiritual, and universal outfits* of the people of their acting repertoire has made their psyche very flexible and their life realization much more realistic, insightful, and loving. They develop *the wisdom of life* that makes them great and the world revered actors.

"Imitation is the best self-renovation!" (Konstantin Stanislavsky)

We need to do the same in life, only *playing our own authentic roles* with a conscious reflection in the mirror of our conscience the harmful or very good roles that we have played so far and that were either scripted for us by the social situations and the people that are much more characterful than us, or by ourselves. *The ability for self-analysis* is essential in life because it puts the right and the left brains in sync and generates the work of *the one-pointed mind - the mind of a personable integrity*. Self-reflection expands our **LOVE BIO-FIELDS** and d creates the atmosphere of synergy with the **TRAJECTORY OF MUTUALLY SHARED LOVE.**

Mind - to - Mind	⟶	*Smile - to – Smile;*
Hug- to - Hug	⟶	*Heart– to -Heart;*
Eyes - to - Eyes	⟶	*Love - to – Love;*
Ears- to - Ears	⟶	*Soul - to – Soul!*

Finally. love is our direct line to the Universal Intelligence, *the Omnipresent God.* When we love, we are immediately connected to the Above and guided by love.

So, Make Wisdom in Love Your Identity Stuff!

23. Don't Let a Dirty Sex Drive Ruin Your Love Life!

(An Inspirational Booster)

Don't let the dirty sex stuff

Rule your love life!

Learn to provide a sex rebuff

Not to let it suck you into the evil gulf

Of disbalance, depression,

Fear, anger, or more sex obsession!

Uncontrolled sex takes minutes or hours,

But resonates into days, months, and years of dirty sprouts!

It deletes time of your love's biz

With its obtrusive trapeze.

Together with money doing its inner split,

It adds the volume of self-guilt!

Don't dream of happiness to come; happiness is your every day's outcome!

Avoid a Cheap Sex Trap; Be in a Strong Moral Wrap!

24. To Soul-Rewind, Be Kind to the Unkind! Be One of a Kind!

In sum, our everyday goal on the emotional front is to peal the layers of despair, fear, and disillusionment from the notion of love and keep it intact in the heart and the mind, without letting them become violent. The reminder again,

The choices we make dictate the love we live!

Obviously, working at a conscious, informed, and committed ***soul-refined love*** requires a lot of self-discipline, will-power, and self-limitations. But such discipline-imposed life rewards us with an amazing feeling of self-uplifting over all the troubles and tribulations of life. We start practicing self-restriction, devoid of self-conviction, self-justification, and blaming another!

It is an accepted fact that with ***self-discipline and a conscious emotional control,*** we start enjoying life **AS IS,** without comparing it to some else's and labelling ourselves as losers. The vastness of knowledge to be obtained and the accomplishments that our enriched and operative intelligence can produce are mind-boggling.

We are becoming wiser, more tolerant, and love imbued, rather.

There is no self-discipline without an emotional self-control. The hardest to master is the ***ability not to hit back the offender and forgive him / her afterwards***, remembering that you are not perfect, either. If you think so, you are growing to be better than them, and it's a great relief.

The ripping effect of kindness is never mindless!

If you monitor your self-growth along the five stages, mentioned above consciously, you will manage ***to integrate yourself into a whole being with a strong personal integrity core.*** You will become kind to the unkind, compassionate, and reserved. You will sure be scanning people more insightfully, and you will always be looking for someone better than you. You will become a **SELF-GURU!** The most destructive mind-set" *I don't care*! would be ousted from your soul. Self-monitoring in the physical, emotional, mental, spiritual, and universal domains will become naturally integrating you and your wisdom of X-raying people for the qualities that you need and value.

Put the left and the right brains in sync; feel but think!

So, upload some character- making inspirational mind-sets against upsets from this book or any other one into your smart phone, and inspire yourself with them *willingly, willfully, and consistently*. Most importantly, have them installed in the front lobes of your brain. Be overly sane!

They will pop up at the right time and boost your inspiration in twine!

It's normal for your spirit to be sagging sometimes due to love problems. Your body is the conduit of vibrations, and it fluctuates in ups and downs. Your pulse can remind of life's rhythm in you.

21-21-21- Life is fun! life is fun! Life is fun!

Auto-inductions will charge the brain with a new *mental-emotional energy of the integrating quality* of self-love and the love for the other.

To succeed in the love bizz; love the One you are with!

Remember, love is not an obligation, and it has nothing to do with the phrases: You must…! You are supposed to… You should…! ***Love is an ability and the Skill*** *that you are developing in yourself consciously and continuously.*

Don't Let the Emotional Carbon Dioxide Twist Your Love Life!

25. Put on the Crown of the King/Queen and Be Serene!

Love is in "the Stream of Consciousness" Flow; Let it Grow!

Love-Emancipation is in Self-Salvation!

(End of the Love Zone Two - Emotional Dimension)

Love Storage Needs a Lot of Knowledge!

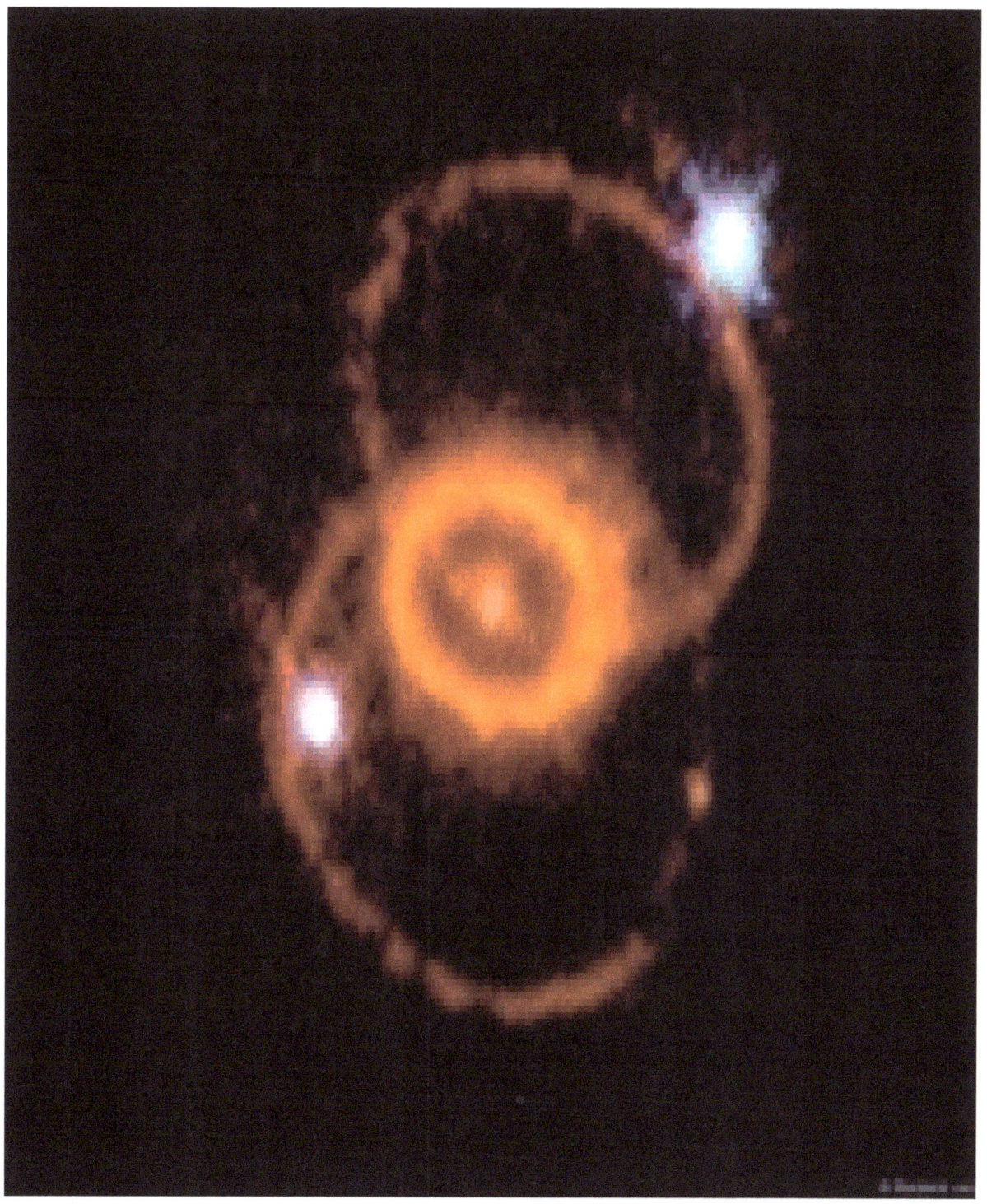

"Be Master of Mind, rather than Mastered by Mind!" *(Zen Philosophy)*

Love Zone Three

(Mental Dimension)

Love

Awareness

Zone

Self- Love
(The Self-Growth Level of Self – Installation)

(Induction for Self-Production)

I Can't Change the Circumstance, but I can change my Attitude to them!

1. Love Stuff Begins with Self-Love!

(Self-Induction for Love Production)

In My Mind,
I am One of a Kind!
I have in me
Spiritual Glee!
I never Whine;
I Shine!

"**Whoever Knows Himself Knows God.**"
(Muhammad)

Love-Refining is in Self-Redefining!

2. Love Intelligence without Negligence

There is no self-perfection without learning! (*See "Living Intelligence or the Art of Becoming!" 2019*) In the mental dimension, **the Holistic Self-Actualization** pyramid is presented by me in five levels as the ten basic **VISTAS OF INTELLIGENCE** that a self-resurrecting person needs to master nowadays. It is outlined in the most general terms below. All the stages are interconnected into onr holistic system that is meant to expand a learner's general outlook and develop his / her indispensable ability *to trace every problem in life or love to its cause.*

10. Universal Intelligence	**Super-Level** of Consciousness
9. Spiritual Intelligence	*(The Universal Dimension)*
8 Social Intelligence	**Macro- Level**
7. Cultural Intelligence	*(The Spiritual Dimension)*
6. Financial Intelligence	**Mezzo-Level**
5. Professional /*Creative* / **Intelligence**	*(The Mental Dimension)*
4. Psychological Intelligence	**Meta- Level**
3 Emotional Intelligence	*(The Emotional Dimension)*
Stage 3	
`2. Language Intelligence	**Mini-Level**
1. General Intelligence *(Self-Genesis)*	*(The Physical Dimension)*

The Spiral of Self-Resurrection in a Fractal Formation:

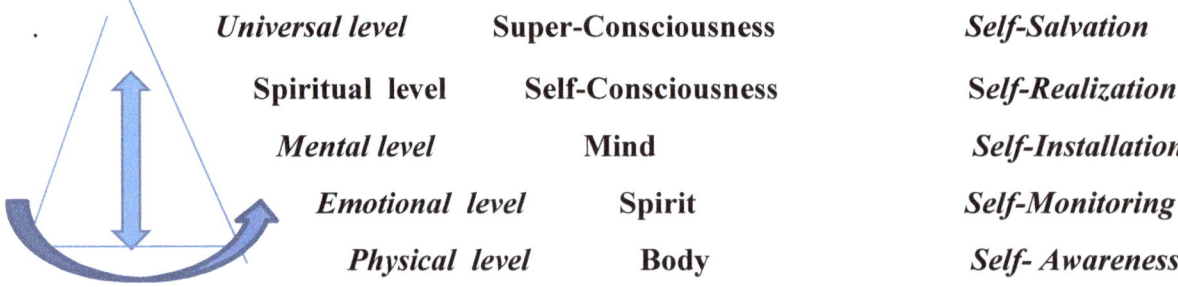

Universal level	Super-Consciousness	*Self-Salvation*
Spiritual level	Self-Consciousness	*Self-Realization*
Mental level	Mind	*Self-Installation*
Emotional level	Spirit	*Self-Monitoring*
Physical level	Body	*Self- Awareness*

Body+ Spirit+ Mind + Self-Consciousness+ Universal Consciousness =

Become a Holistically Developed, Love-Enhanced Self!

3. Love is the Rainbow of Enlightened Self-Consciousness!

At the mental level of love education, we need to continue *raising self-consciousness knowingly and consciously.* Every stage of self-growth is the stage of awareness and accumulation of new knowledge, but since we systematize our being and discipline our thoughts, words, and emotions, it's vital to develop the habit of a quick **SELF-SCANNING** in the *physical, emotional, mental, spiritual, and universal* realms of life every evening to assess the level of your life awareness and self-improvement in it. The Internet has an avalanche of information that should be sifted for its validity to raise our *electro-magnetic vibrations* that make it possible for the right people to get magnetized to us love-wise. Nikola Tesla said,

"Life is the electro-magnetic force, and we are electro-people."

To meet the challenges of the new times, we need to educate ourselves in **all the vistas of intelligence, presented above at least at the dilettante level** to be able to accumulate the electro-magnetic energy by uniting the heart and the mind in the process of **LOVE MAGNITIZATION**, meant to restore *the Merkabah's electro-magnetic circuit of love* that is disconnected in us now..

The scientific community is discovering now the ties to our mental and physical health on the cellular level, relating it to raising our self-consciousness and *purifying the second brain – the gut.* According to the Chinese scientist, Mantak Chia, our digestive tract can have a huge impact on the rest of the body – including the brain. His discoveries give a new meaning to the statements:

<u>*We need a lot of guts to sustain the life' s buts!*</u>

There are a lot of situations in life when being gutsy helps to withstand the challenges, proving Dr. Chia's idea that the second brain plays a great role in the character formation. People often justify their weaknesses with a common " ***But, I* …**" There is a great response to such justification of wrongdoing in English -" ***But me no buts*!**" It is also a case of the linguistic phenomenon of *inversion* in English, when one part of speech can be inverted into another. Likewise, we need *to invert our weaknesses into personable strength of our guts*. - our second brain. We need **LOVE GUTS** in a relationship, too because there is always the tendency in a relationship for one partner to control the other To be able to turn any conflicting situation to the advantage of both, *joint love skills need to be developed* on the basis of the love codes that have been ascertained by the couple.

There are millions of amazingly talented people around us, and the **TANDEM** of their **LOVE SKILLS** inspires them to create the breathtaking buildings in architecture, the most harmonious pieces of music, mesmerizingly beautiful art designs, and new discoveries in science, motivated by the desire for a gutsy self-expression.

> *The talent of love is now a boundless technological stuff!*

Amazingly, the timeless world wisdom that *"the way to a man's heart goes through his gut!"* is more than accurate, too. We find a loving rapport with the subject of love on the intellectual level at a dinner table. We also exchange ideas and pick someone's brains at business luncheons. The family peace is the always restored by a good family dinner that unites the family and harmonizes it.

To conclude, an intellectual charm of a man or a woman is as strong a magnet in a love relationship as a physical attractiveness. Two popular Russian proverbs point out the importance of the mental level of a love partner in making the choice of the One for marriage.

> *If a man is better looking than a monkey, but is intelligent, he is the best catch for you. // Don't be carried away by a woman's looks. See how she talks.*

To Develop a Loving Gut,

Become Overly Smart!

Turn your Thinking Time into the Thinking Love!

"Be Master of Mind, rather than Mastered by Mind!" *(Zen Philosophy)*

4. Love Realism without Skepticism

The path of every period of life leaves a flowing print, like a jet does. ***It's the body of the memory that is stored in the sub-conscious mind.*** Interestingly, neuro-science claims that the main print can be left in the brain by a strong imprint of a happy / unhappy love that we all experience in time and space and that is stored in the compartment of wisdom that is enriched with age.

Wisdom is a simple anatomy of knowledge!

The quality of the love wisdom imprints and their depth in the brain curves are determined by the **QUALITY OF LOVE** that we are granted from the Above. However, it so happens that the divine love gift is wasted, neglected, or betrayed. People appear to be unable to handle love and preserve it. Ignorance remains " *the worst enemy of the humanity."(Albert Einstein)*

Like everything else in life, a love relationship needs order and cleaning of the residue of the *physical, emotional, mental, spiritual, and universal imprints in the sub-conscious mind.* Processing your innermost feelings through this ***mind+ heart cleansing grid*** develops the love **Habits +Skills** connection, or the **Form + Content** unity indispensable for a long-term relationship. *(See Part One,12)* Regrettably, it appears that only those people that are in the flow of new scientifically- backed up information evolve. Others remain love and life uneducated and uninformed, and therefore, their relationships are stuck in the vicious circle of repeating the same mistakes and. A Chinese proverb says,

> ***"Teachers open the door, but you must enter yourself."***

Love education is the most important part of the self-growing process It must be taken seriously, without a religious warning of committing a sin or a banal justification, *"**No one is perfect**."* Being human, we can also be inwardly divine. The Zen philosophy says,

"Water that is too Pure has no Fish."

5. The Authenticity of Self is in the Spiritualized Love Cell!

The reality of love proves that you can be successful in the love scenario if it is written by the author – **You!** Take off the mask of your assumed main role and peel off the layers of the action roles. Start self-evolving in the State of love from the Above!

Self-growth is love growth!

No empty, wasteful love expectations and love frustrations should be in the way.. It means that life pendulum has stopped making swings from the negative to the positive movements. It has been stabilized in the neutral *Zero position.* **The LAW OF BALANCE** will start ruling your love, based on the newly formed love habits and skills..

" Nothing so needs reforming as our habits." (Mark Twain)

It's never too late to change the ritual of a regular birthday celebration to an **INNER ELATION** with self-transformation. Celebrate a beautiful change that is going on inside and that puts your *Merkabah circuit* back to work in its mind+ heart love generating unity. Also, stop having compromises with your soul. *Life will ruin any indecent goal!* Be true to your **AUTHENTIC SELF** that you have re-discovered. Use the auto-induction below be your ever-helping hand,

I am my best friend; I am my beginning and my end!

Say only good, positive things about yourself. Do not criticize yourself or express your doubts to anyone Don't try to even your own personal spiritual level with the level of others to please them or to let them think that they are not the only ones that experience problems in life.

"Be the thing in itself!" (Hegel) Be your authentic Self!

Also, be silent about others. People build up wrong images about the lives of other people, often destroying them with the comments that they hear from others about themselves.

The same happens when you comment on your love relationship. The level of *exaggeration and self-justification* distorts the real situation in the minds of the listeners, and they come up with wrong advice that many people, lacking self-confidence follow. **LOVE PRIVATELY!** Doubts are the signals of the mind's disconnection with the heart.

Listen to your heart and make it smart!

Human life is an enigma

That leaves on everyone a moral stigma

Of petty passions and vices

Of endless desires, garnished with sexual spices.

This enigma, though, is movable

And as we mature becomes removable!

But to clean up your moral set,

You need to have a spiritual bet

To will your love more

And stop being a desire whore!

To spread your spiritual wings,

Don't let others pull your emotional strings!

Only Intellect and Intuition provide the Right Solution's Submission!

6. Not to Love-Drain, Have the Love Police in the Brain!

Our society is possessed with a love frenzy *"to get laid."* It is always the result of an unconscious reaction to libido excitement. To tame this frenzy and engage the mind in a sex provoking situation, you must **learn to control your emotions at will**. We must bring *the Art of Love* into anything, and love education is the **ALMA-MATER** of it.

Habits + Grace+ Skills are the life - enhancing wheels!

To mobilize your cognitive resources, put yourself together and stabilize your emotions. It's hard to be thoughtful and emotionally balanced when you are love frustrated and distraught, when the hurt of being neglected or deceived is beyond endurance. However, the inner mentor is the true love's rater! Intuition is your **EMOTIONAL GUARDIAN** that you need to employ in every situation and that will help you instill the basics of the *Emotional Diplomacy* in the brain. *(See "Soul-Refining")* It's never late to start doing it by learning the ethics of behavior, good manners, and self-presentation in public. These skills are part of the love skills that must be instilled in kids.

Not to self-drain, we need to install love police in the brain!

We should be aware of our feelings at a certain moment and take action if we forget due an overwhelmingly hurtful reason, who we are.. When we put ourselves together, we are ready to mobilize our cognitive resources., maintain the focus of aware attention, and **"resist, reject, and reform"** an inner de-form.

Love is the only feeling that helps inner reformation effortlessly. Unfortunately, we live in the pretty shallow time. So, we need to dig down deeper than before to reach the sense of authenticity and sincerity within *Sadh guru says, "The level of inclusiveness that love provides goes beyond the physical essence. It's mental."*

Staying on the Path of Transformation is a Self-Revelation!

7. To Be Highly Love Rated, Become More Love-Acculturated!

The cutting-edge tech and the research on health informatics have put women at a higher place in the sensing ranks of love and loving. The burdens of chronic diseases and aging, as well as men's mental and emotional stability are increasingly falling to women's care now because young women grow up with technology.

"Women are looking to tech to have a role – to make things better."(Elizabeth Mynatt)

And women do make things better in many spheres of life, space exploration included. Other than that, women have a much better developed intuition, strategic thinking, more stress endurance, and much better manners than men. Science has it that *"men tend to excel in shorter term, goal-oriented situations, while women are better in longer-term circumstances."(National Geographic, June,2019)*

No wonder, behind every successful man is a woman!

But, most importantly, women are more interpersonally sensitive, more communicative, and more **LOVE-ACCULTURATED.** We need <u>to give love back its manners and a romantic, knight-like flavor</u> that is based on the mind + heart unity This link is the engine of the love car that wouldn't be driving if the <u>**Love Diplomacy**</u> parts were broken. Unfortunately, **LOVE MANNERS** are now in gutters!

To be more love-emphatic, learn to be more love-diplomatic!

Being rude, abusive, insulting and downright dirty must be totally unacceptable in every sphere of our social life that is overloaded with profanity and most disgusting manners.

Having good manners today means being able to stand somebody's bad manners!

Love is suffocating in the company of hefty, squinting, inflexible, mind-barren guys that would rather masturbate than make a move to win the woman of their fantasy with the intellect, not the body parts and the shape of the abs.

Inspiring and sculpturing ourselves in five levels, we are developing the most important skill - **the Skill of Life.** We learn to put the mind and heart in sync, *making the mind and the heart smart!*

<u>MIND + SPIRIT + HEART + SELF-CONSCIOUSNESS + SUPER-CONSCIOUSNESS</u>
A Self-Refined Fractal of You!

Thus, we'll boost our self-power to build up a more meaningful and creative, and refined life, we'll become kinder, more compassionate, and considerate people.

The goal for our education is to develop in each child a much more **ACCULTURATED PERSONALITY** - in t*he* **Physical Culture** *(more knowledge about the systems of the body and the ways of its better functioning);* the **Emotional Culture** *(skills in managing emotions and acquiring the habits in Emotional Diplomacy),* the **Mental Culture** *(getting rid of the limited or distorted vision of the world and obtaining a much wider outlook of the world and it and);* the **Spiritual Culture** *(following the self-growth messages of the religious leaders and practicing what they preach consciously),* and the **Universal Culture** *(knowledge about the new technology and its explorative perspectives in going beyond the terrestrial boundaries)*

Let's replace the banners on our manners!

"The Road is Mastered by the One who's Walking."

(Dalai Lama)

Love Diplomacy hasn't died, and it Must Be Revived!

8. The Love Gravity Connection is Grounded in Love Reflection!

The enemy of any relationship has always been cheating. It has become a commonly discussed thing in almost every dire love-hate situation that demands first a thorough analysis of the cause-effect character in every of the life dimensions. *What has been wrong in your love life physically, emotionally, mentally, and spiritually?* Give yourself time to ponder on the reasons of the love breach without discussing it with anyone.

Be sincere and objective with yourself first!

Love wisdom teaches us that men tend to be unfaithful with their bodies, but women with their minds. The first is a natural thing and can and should be faced in a rational way, while the second one is a serious warming for the relationship that, most certainly, will soon die. Women need to always remember that *men are heterogeneous creatures*. They *"think about love only at time"(S. Maugham)* and they love with their eyes. Seeing a sexy, beautiful woman that is approachable is hard to resist and even though the excitement is irresistible, it still has a logical end. *Women are the same in nature!*

The problem is, at the beginning of an affair, a man compares a new woman to his wife or a girlfriend *in favor of a new woman*. She seems to be more desirable, attractive, understanding, and kind. Unfortunately, on top of the complications that cheating involves, the first woman often takes an attacking, revengeful position, cutting the **UMBELICAL CORD** of the mutually raised love then and there. Time passes and the man starts feeling *the gravitating force of the previous relationship*, his family life, the kids, and the usual equilibrium of his **CLEAR CONSCIENCE**. Now he processes his previous life in the heart and mind *in favor of the first woman.*

The back lashing gets into a reverse action!

Unfortunately, the deserted woman had already re=programmed her cells. If she were a little more self-confident, patient, and self-loving, she would've have enjoyed the time of the man's realization of what he had lost and a happy make up would've enlightened the family.

None of us is perfect in such a situation, and the rule of wisdom should save us from the most unpleasant consequences

Being imperfectly perfect in any life situations saves us from frustration!

The gravitational force of the love that had been rooted in the minds and the hearts of both partners for the time of their life together can always bring love back. The family life gets restored, kids are not emotionally distraught, commonly built homes are not left, hearts are not broken. Love will continue blossoming! Give it another chance!

<u>**Life is going on, and it's great in its renewed form!**</u>

All it takes is the correct behavior of a woman and *her knowledge of a man's psychology*. It's, of course, paramount not to constantly remind each other of the wrongdoing afterwards, thus generating a new breach of trust. The idea of a woman's wisdom and patience in a relationship is wonderfully presented by an Italian writer, *Arturo Vivante* in his small, but a very insightful story about a husband having an affair and the wife acting in the wisest way possible.

The story is called " **Can-Can**"*, and it tells us about the husband who decided to go for a ride in the evening. The wife who counted on his help with their two small kids, did not question him where he was going and why. When the husband was going to leave, she was playing with the son who asked her to do the can-can. At this point, the husband started wondering why she did not ask him anything but danced in a very sexy way. Anyway, he headed to a lake house to meet Sarah, his wife's friend whom he had been having an affair with for quite some time. The story ends when Sarah, lying in his arms and sensing some detachment from him, asked him what he was thinking of.*

*The man said, "**I'm thinking of someone dancing can-can**. – " **Thank goodness**," sighed Sarah, "**I was worried you were thinking about your wife**." The ironic ending is indicative of the shaky feelings of a man and very confident behavior of his wife who practically ended his affair without even knowing about it.*

To Succeed in the Love Bizz,

Love the One You are with!

If You are Wise, you are on Top of Love Paradise!

(Pictures by Fred Cronin)

Love Branch Connectedness is in Self-Reflectiveness!

9. Self-Patronage in Love

It's great if your spiritual growth is inseparable with the growth of your loved one's self-consciousness and your mutual consideration for *the mind+ heart unity* that binds you together. But don't impose your self-improvement on your partner. *Just demonstrate it, be a love role model!* Your kids will imitate you in their love relationship later.

The synergy of the Love Space is a delicate case!

The magnetic charging of the common (home / work) space with grace must be conducted in the most unpretentious, genuine, and non-declarative way. Every one of us is born with a dream of love, but many cut the wings of that dream and do not let it fly in the corrupted space of a partner's place.

<u>We truly are who we love and how!</u>

Life proves that the best kids are raised by the parents of wisdom and grace! Remember the ever-actionable rule, " *Love is not words; love is action!* Magnetize yourself and the object of your love in every cell with your love. Personal love magmatism should become your main" ism!" It is an unbelievably rewarding feeing when you start genuinely perceiving that your soul space is being gradually, but surely filled up with *inner grace that obliterates the vices* that are like viruses in your biological computer. Your self-respect grows.

Self-Refining is pure living without cheating and lying!

Regrettably, the present-day kids are more sexually oriented, computer games pre-programmed, and cheap love vision-obsessed, rather than in any way spiritually intellectualized and self-realization wise. *Only with the conscious spiritual intelligence at work, can one stop being a jerk!* Naturally, spiritual maturation and self-transformation should start growing with "*the Apple Tree*", so that "*the apples*" from your family tree did not fall far from it and got rotten.

To generate the Inner Bliss, become a More Contentious Mister or Miss!

10. Being Content with the One that God put on your Path is a Must!

Science has it that *we tend to couple with someone of the opposite brain dominance*, so that left-brained types tend to mate with right brainers. As the Chinese physicians say, *the equilibrium of the yin and yang principles* results in longevity and the inner peace of love in the beauty of life and the gift of it every day. The possibility of meeting and marrying your missing second half is very slim, but if you make the choice of the One, having inwardly scanned him / her through the five levels holistically, the chances become much stronger.

There is no whole-brain conformity in many cases!

Maybe your wife isn't interested in facts and figures, but she might be a keen observer of the real world, able to raise your kids in love. *Taming the mood swings and impulsiveness* is a very important point to consider. Unfortunately, we forget that being emotionally - reserved is needed not only at work, but mostly at home.

The climate of your life with its different seasons depends on how you feel at home.

People may be different in their characters brain-wise, but spiritually, people tend to mate with the ones who have the same spiritual values. The cosmic Law of Attraction works on the spiritual level, and in this respect, the lack of spiritual conformity is reflected in the wisdom: *A husband and wife are of one devil's type"*

Also, try to live morally and responsibly to be always ready to honestly declare the British rule in a new way, fortifying your love life with a happy conviction: *"My love / home is my castle!"*

It is difficult to build the love castle, but not let it be a sandcastle! We all experience a wonderful peace inside knowing that we are loved and protected by love. Induct yourself and your loved ones with:

I am Happy, no matter what; Happiness is My Full-Time Job!

11. "The Stream of Consciousness" Technique is the Love Peak!

A great American writer *James Joyce,* in his masterpiece *"Ulysses"* uses a famous literary technique, known as *"the stream pf consciousness"* that, in my understanding, we need to master, too. James Joyce thought of mind as a constantly changing flow that, in fact, it is, being part of the Universal Stream of Consciousness.

To live and to be in harmony with life means to be in *the Field of Consciousness* that is in us and around us. Everything will happen according to its divine plan. But we are forming our life ourselves and should always remember about it. When we are in the flow of the Universal stream of consciousness, that we have no control of, the right person appears at the right place and at the right time *only if we deserve it!* Unfortunately, many people live unconsciously, by inertia, and therefore, they get disconnected with love that constitutes *the unity of the form and the content* of life in its inseparable, holistically magnetized Oneness:

Thoughts and emotions flow illogically in our minds, but we need to put them in order to change the inner working of the mind and resolve the problems that inevitably appear in life due to our unconsciously led relationships. We absolutely need to *make your living and loving conscious!* Then our self-growth will be unfolding in its entirety, and the inner misery and the inertia of living will bake out.

The ability to balance the thinking and X-ray the thoughts and emotions for their validity in our life, thus cleaning the stream of our self-consciousness, by the paradigm *Synthesis – Analysis – Synthesis* (*Part Two, 11)* is essential in love relationship for the sense of awareness that you need to enrich in yourself all your life.. In other words, we need to provide congenial conditions for love growth and sustaining for years.

Generalize–Internalize– Personalize!
Be Love Wise!

12. Your Radiate What You Emanate!

Refocus Your Being on the New Paradigm of Thinking, Feeling, Speaking, and Seeing!

Learn Acting Without Reacting!

Systematize - Actualize - Strategize! Be overly Wise!

(Observe your universal, spiritual, mental, emotional, and physical code. Mold Yourself, Mold!)

Put the Shield of Faith on Your Love's Interface!

13. Love-Sanity is in Self-Gravity!

A good relationship between a man and a woman always generates the **LOVE GRAVITY** that must become the goal of any committed relationship, especially a healthy family life. Love gravity is growing in its density and the magnetic power at the **micro, meta, mezzo, macro, and super levels**, or in the *physical, emotional, mental, spiritual, and universal levels* of our common life and make love worth preserving in any dire situations that a couple might face in life..

It's our obligation to monitor love in these levels without frustration.

The gravity of love keeps the family together for years on end, and it must be consciously geared, nurtured, and revered. Taking love to another level does not mean to just get to live together, or to consider marriage as a pushing option, without any *"what ifs"*.

The gravity of love is a consciously developed feeling of belonging!

I remember a very insightful tale by Hans Christian Anderson, called **"Elsa."** My dad read and explained it to me so well that I had never had **"The Elsa complex"** since that day.

The tale has it that there lived a young girl who was dreaming to get married. Finally, the groom with his mates came to her home and asked her father for her hand. The father asked Elsa to go down to the vine cell and bring a bottle of vine to treat the suitor. When Elsa was in the vine cell, picking the bottle, her eyes fell on the ax, hanging on the wall. She started picturing what would happen if she got married, had a child, the child came down to the cell, and the ax fell on his head and killed him. While she was "musing" about life in the "What if?" fashion, the groom and his mates were gone.

The **"What if"** concept ruins love gravity and de-magnetizes love in its core. Don't discharge your bio-battery of love with doubts and fears. Be overly wise and love re-vised.

Be a Soldier of Love, not Just a Love Dove!

14. Commitment is Me; Commitment is My Philosophy!

At the new technological times of the up-coming **SUPER-INTELLIGENCE, we** will probably be able to upload skills and abilities. The time will come when we 'll embrace both aspects of our existence - *internal and external*, or personal and social. existence. Meanwhile, being conscious is being self-aware here and there!

The Risk Zone that you have managed to leave with your commitment to a relationship or marriage may quickly turn into *the Zone of Expectation* and hopes that are never justified. The other half will not change and commit to your love unconditionally, unless you do!

A person can commit only to being Soul-Fit!

There are many self-help books that sketch a plan of action on the path of success and human relationships. They may be compelling on paper, but utterly impractical in life because they are holistic in their structure and therefore, they lack the character-building system. Other than that, these books do not talk about the necessity *to raise your self-consciousness* - the goal that is above any other.

Everything becomes possible if you make self-growth irreversible!

Regrettably, many people do not even think about *committing to self-transformation*, and therefore, they cannot make themselves committed to a job, a family, or long-lasting love. They may be committed to exercising daily to be more physically fit, but to *commit to better living and loving* is not there. So, their life is a torture and despair when committing is devoid of repair. Only *the one who does not sin in the world is of a perfect thought.* As Carl Yung teaches us,

"When you choose the behavior, you choose the consequences."

It's incredibly hard to commit to a tedious, uninteresting job, to a woman / man that you do not love and do not respect any more. We do it, anyway, justifying ourselves with all kinds of reasons that eventually lead us to the break of the commitment with a much more hurtful result. We cannot get out of any problematic situations because we constantly doubt, filling our consciousness with *dis-harmonious vibrations* that we generate daily with our hateful and uncontrolled thoughts and words. "*I hate it*!" is constantly heard here and abroad!

Eliminate the words of hate from your mind storage and love voltage!

It's only when we remain true to ourselves and to the commitment *to retain the health of the soul* that we can resist the cacophony of the inner spiritual, mental, emotional, and physical chaos. Companies, cheating, drugs, or alcohol only suck us in deeper. The inner sounding becomes low and non-resistant to evil that's always persistent.

We stop shining from inside with kindness, care, compassion, and consideration – the qualities that are innate in us but are under the layers of impersonal indifference, lies, and *soul-twisting for years on end.* Should this happen to you, auto-suggestively induct yourself with healthier fluctuations of light, sensible convictions, and beliefs. Help your sub-conscious mind follow the conscious one.

Love has a neurological basis; to think and love is one stuff!

That's why the commitment to peeling off the negative layers of fears and doubts is paramount. No wonder we call psychiatrists *"Shrinks"*. They help us shrink emotionally by cutting off the mental and emotional vampires on our *love body.* It is desperately needed, and it must preferably be done by a person himself / herself.

Be committed to the auto-suggestive self-help first and foremost and remember the mind-set: *I am my best friend; I am my beginning and my end ! I never whine – I shine!*

Only a strong personality can create a new personal reality!

Self-Luminosity that's emitting from Thee is your Love Protection Glee!

15. "The Hypnosis of Social Conditioning"

But "the hypnosis of social conditioning" *(Deepak Chopra)*
Is still affecting my reasoning!
    I become a mob-driven particle,
    In a socially conditioned article.
My thinking is blurred and messed,
And I become totally obsessed
    With worries and concerns
    About my problems and deforms.
My personal life
Gets in strife,
    And I become driven by fear
    That results in love smear.
I am no longer life-mesmerized;
I am life-paralyzed!
    I come back to being Me
    Only if I cut the cord with the conditioning love sea!
Only if I disconnect my emotional set
From the social network web!
    Thus, I ascend my individual cell
    To the Universal Spell!

Freed from the Social Spell, Love Makes Sense Again!

Let's Marvel at the Boundless Talent of a Love-filled Human Mind!

(An unbelievable Chinese confectioner- Zhou Yi)

From the Time of Creation, a Woman is the Main Inspiration!

16. Self-Sufficiency Attracts More than Sexuality!

At the mental level, women pay the crucial role in men's life because the love of a woman has become the platform of a man's self-realization and self-sufficiency. The statement, **behind every successful man is a woman"** is a one-way street, though, because behind every successful woman is herself!

She is her own best friend!

There are zillions of examples of men that became inspired by the woman they loved. **Women gravitate to the mind of the man more than to the sexual strength** of a much less intelligent man, and the more interesting and magnetic a man's dedication to his goal is, the more attracted a woman is and the more helpful she is in charging his **physical, emotional, mental, and spiritual potential**. A woman should see her mission in launching the man of her admiration to his victory, and the person who is overwhelmingly proud of such a man is always the woman behind him.

Unfortunately, men after having accomplished the desired goal and after having acknowledged the role of the woman behind him on this path, **often get back into the risk zone again,** being carried away by the physical magnetism of a younger woman, often ruining their personalities and losing their creative drive.

A successful woman, on the contrary, having relied on herself on the chosen path becomes much stronger in spirit and **obtains a true physical, emotional, and mental maturation.** A successful woman is self-confident, self-sufficient, and self-reliant. She is reasonably wise and uses her femininity as an irresistible device. **No wonder, men gravitate to strong women as flies get attracted by light.** The charge of the mind + heart is always magnetizing at that!

Love Gravitates to the Personal Magnetism's Space!

17. Keep Your Spiritual Form in a in the Dignified Uniform!

Most definitely, the growth of intellect is the reflection of your inner growth too. *"If you change your intelligence you change your life!" (Leo Vygotsky)* The higher self-consciousness of a person, the more capable of love he /she is. Forgiveness in this respect is the process of purifying consciousness from the pollutants of bitterness, envy, anger, and hatred. **Mind cannot change the brain, only you can!** The soul that resonates into the rays of kindness, passion and compassion warms up the soul's space in his /her Merkabah link. But, it's vital not to separate yourself from the general flow of the reality and see yourself from a bird's eye view. **Synthesis-Analysis-Synthesis!**

Generalize - Personalize -Actualize. Be strategically wise!

People do not know that they are ignorant in all five levels of life. The **KNOW-HOW** of the physical fitness is a maigre part of the knowledge that one needs to be in the flow of *the physical, emotional, mental, spiritual, and universal evolution.* True love is inseparable with the emotional, intellectual and spiritual maturity that is a ***holistic vision of your inner and outer worlds*** without being indoctrinated by any religious limitations and ethical norms. *Sadhguru,*

"Spirituality is getting out of the circle of religion into the circle of life."

You must know your physical state and take a good care of your health *(the physical level)*, control your emotional state and be always positively-charged *(the emotional level)*, enrich your intelligence with new knowledge in its unstoppable flow *(the mental level)* deepen your spiritual maturity *(the spiritual level),* and finally, be aware of the constant growth of your unifying self-consciousness *(the universal level.)* We all know that *o*nce a person opens his mouth and says something stupid or dirty, love evaporates first from the mind and then from the heart expediently.

Don't Complain or Blame; Be Subliminally Sane!

18. Take Care of the Gene of Your Mind's Hygiene!

I have mentioned above that *love oasis has a neurological basis!* Don't waste it in the argumentative races! No wonder, the latest discoveries in Neurology prove that the seat of love is not the heart; it's the mind. *"An ordinary man and an enlightened man are as different as that of a snake and a giraffe."* (R. H. Blyth)

<u>MIND + SPIRIT + HEART + SELF-CONSCIOUSNESS + SUPER-CONSCIOUSNESS</u> = **The Soul-Refined You!**

Spiritual maturation of such holistic value is the process of constant self-control, discipline and self-reflection. It's never enough to just pray or meditate. Our body has an amazing storage of memory that records colors, smells, and words. An accidental sexual entanglement messes up the memory of love and often obliterates it because the link between the heart and the mind gets broken.

The result of this unconscious process is the breakage of the neurological foundation for love, or the love established **MIND + BRAIN** unity. The Merkabah circle of life is, in fact, the *neuroplasticity at work.* Dr. Joe. Dispenza in his very powerful talks on You Tube calls on us to *"recondition the brain to a new mind."*

If we reprogram the brain with new values, beliefs, and love standards, if we change the circle of our friends, the places that we frequent, the books that we read, the music that we listen to, and the thoughts that the brain generates will be much more constructive, the love relationships will become much deeper, and our lives will be much more enjoyable. *Self-reflection is a progressive discovery of self-imperfection.* Our mind is generating a new reality, and we are up-dating it, based on the new, technologically enhanced experience.

To Enrich your Inner Personal Store, Will Your Life More!

19. Conquer the Mouth with Love Wows!

With the Umbilical Cord of Love, we are connected to Love from the Above! The wows that we give carry the energy of love that we get when we **_verbally keep our wows_**, watching the mouth. Induct ten of them out loud and try to follow them. **We are what we say!**

1. Protect your mind! Delete bad thoughts and unclutter the feelings. Use a lot of auto-suggestive injections to be always brain sharp and love-.

Don't assume the negative thought - perfume!

2. Protect your mouth! Mean what you say and say what you mean!!

Foul words are love insanity warts!

3. Protect your body! Never harm or pollute your body! Do not destroy the inner rhythm of the body, its harmonious music of health.

To be love-fit, be neat!

4. Protect your heart! Make your mind kind and your heart smart! Deny yourself the luxury to react, be on a control response track!

Learn the art of seeing with your heart!

5. Protect your eyes! Clean your sight from envy, lust, and ugliness.

Eyes are the mirrors of the soul; they self-console!

6. Protect your ears! Don't let gossip, foul language, and bad stories destroy your love.

7. *Protect your spirit!* Don't be a low pole or a sad sack on the love track!

8. Protect your Soul! Don't put a long face on your love's interface!

9. Protect your Self-Image! Love yourself first to be able to love others!

10. Make a deal with yourself; remove every evil spell!

Avoid a Comparison Trap; Be in a Unique Yourself Wrap!

20. Only Independence of the Spirit will Love-Inspirit!

Finally, concluding the mental level of love revision, allow me to remind you that the hardest of all virtues to acquire on the path of Self-Transformation **is** *the independence of thinking, speaking, feeling, and acting!* Life and love are organized on the mental level, and consciously perceived independence charges the inner core of a person with **PERSONAL MAGNETISM.**

An independent person cannot be part of a divisive group of any political or social nature with dubious, arguable, and ruinous standpoints. He / she is self-sufficient, strong in his /her convictions, and, therefore, self-reliant. He /she is aware of his / her self-worth! Inner independence is a true luxury of the spirit!

<u>*The most interesting person on Earth is the One of self-worth!*</u>

Such people can love, and they are the makers of life! My favorite verse comes to mind here. These are the words of a great Russian poet, *Alexander Blok*, in my translation, and I consistently quote them in every of the five books on self-creation and a new personality growth.

> *"I want to desperately live:*
>
> *To eternalize what can be seen,*
>
> *To celebrate the unforeseen,*
>
> *To humanize the irreversible,*
>
> *And to realize the Impossible!*

"Man's Main Task in Life is to give Birth to Himself." *(Erich Fromm)*

(End of the Zone of Self-Awareness - Mental Level)

Love Zone Four
Spiritual Dimension

Self-Sufficiency Zone

(Faith and Inner Grace)

Self-Growth level - Self-Realization

Put the Shield of Faith on Your Love's Interface!

Love will Ever Be Alive if We come to Grips with the Beauty of Life!

("White Lilies", Claude Monet)

"Consciously Perceived Beauty Will Save the World!" (Nickolas Roerich)

1. *Your Love Wings are in God's Ins!*

Faith is Love's Base!

-- -- -- -- -- -- --

In my mind, I am One of a kind!
There wasn't, there isn't,
There won't ever be
Anyone like Me!

(Auto-Induction for Self-Production)

In My Thought,
I Am Married to God!

2. To Deserve Your Very Best, Be on the Spiritual Quest!

In this book, I keep presenting self-growth in love as the path of spiritual maturation consequentially in the *physical, emotional, mental, spiritual, and universal* dimensions. This process is a life-long journey of two steps forward and, one step back that allows you to take a general view at life and yourself in it. It's the process of constant X-Raying of your inner Self in every level consciously and objectively to detect the problems at the right place and at the right time! Love is the state of the highest vibratory fest of being the best.

Life is going on, and you are its unique form!

Every book on Self-Resurrection *("For the Reader to Consider")* has many inspirational mind-sets and boosters that you can upload into your smart phone and use when your mood sags or your enthusiasm on the path of self-transformation fails you. Keep challenging yourself with being calmer, more balanced, intelligent, emotionally controlled, and self-reliant. Watch yourself from the outside, and be content with what you think, say, feel, and do **NOW,** not in the past.

Don't look at yourself in the past; let the past pass!

It's self-degrading to be always unearthing the past or blaming anyone for wrong doings consistently. Unfortunately, it's a bad habit that is harbored in the subconscious mind of many of us. Enjoy the state of being content with life and cherish yourself for the consistency that you demonstrate. *Your spiritual growth is the core of the love magnetism in you!* It is the state of love for yourself and the manifestations of love around. You will be able to simplify your perception of life to the point when every life's moment becomes a consciously appreciated gift.

Your Soul's Work is Praying and a Regular Self-Talk!

3. Spiritual Maturity Guarantees Your Love's Security!

We are trying to explain life and love through religion, philosophy, and Esoterica. But it appears now that we are living now in *the virtual computer matrix,* structured by the Universal Mind that we all call God. Even though we declared love to be God-granted, the present-day direction of love is *from bottom to top* of the holistic paradigm of Self-Creation while the direction of **Love from the Above** has an opposite trajectory-: *from top to bottom* of a person's spiritual growth.

Universal Level	**Oneness**
Spiritual level	**Grace**
Mental level	**Mind**
Emotional level	**Spirit**
Physical level	**Body**

When the two minds and hearts share common knowledge about *the evolutionary development* of life, when they respect each other's *spiritual standards* and the values in which they were raised, when their minds click on *the intellectual level*, the magnetically-charged love attraction will be enhanced *emotionally*, and love will finally culminate into a passionate self-expression on the *physical level.*

Marriages are truly made in Heaven!

Such spiritual magnetism will help love to sustain any troubles and tribulations for years on end. ***That's the spiritual direction of love from the Above!*** This is not to say that love that starts with an uncontrolled physical attraction has no hope, but its spiritually enhanced route will be much more challenging, and, unfortunately, it is not sustainable for many people.

Love Growing is a Creative Process of Self-Molding!

4. *Self-Salvation is in Love Maturation!*

I see a sure parallel of the **FIVE CYCLES OF BEING**, listed above *with a famous parable of Jesus Christ,* told to his disciples. I take the liberty to interpret it below as our five main stages in life. **The wisdom of this parable is a great lesson for us to learn.**

The Route of Self-Resurrection is to be considered in love-formation, too.

5. **Super** - *Universal Level*   *Self-Salvation* -   Oneness with God Zone
4. **Macro** - *Spiritual Level*   *Self-Realization* –   Self-Sufficiency Zone
3. **Mezzo** - *Mental Level*   *Self-Installation* –   Love Awareness Zone
2. **Meta** - *Emotional Level*   *Self-Monitoring* –   Breach of Trust Zone
1. **Mini** - *Physical Level*   Self-*Awareness* –   Risk Love Zone

The Parable of Timeless Wisdom

1. The First Period of Life - <u>Youth –Self-Awareness</u> (Age 16-21- the age of romanticizing of life. – **The Risk Love Zone**)

I am walking down the road.

I don't see the hole in it.

I fall into the hole.

-*"It's not my fault!"*

It takes a long time to get out of the hole.

---

2. The Second Period of Life – <u>Self-Monitoring</u> (Age 21-35 – *the* age of conformism and obtaining emotional self-control -**Breach of Trust Zone)**

I am walking down the same road.

I see the hole, but I fall into it again.

- How come I'm in the same hole. Maybe, it's my fault."

It takes much less time to get out.

3. The Third Period of Life – Self-Installation (Age 35- 45 - the age of intellectual growth and the realistic perception of life. – **Love-Awareness Zone**)

I am walking down the same road.

I see the hole., however, I fall into it again.

"It's definitely my fault!"

I get out of the hole in no time.

----

4. The Fourth Period of Life – Spiritual Evolution – Self-Realization - (Age 45- 65 – the age of reason, life-awareness and spiritual maturity. – **Self-Sufficiency Zone***)*

I am walking down the same road.

I see the hole.

I go around it!

----

5. The Fifth Period of Life – Self-Salvation (Age 65-85 + the age of wisdom and the universality of thinking – **Oneness with God Zone***)*

I am walking down the same road.

I see the hole.

I take another road!

Drive though the time and space with knowledge and grace on your Life's Interface!

"Nothing so Needs Reforming as Our Habits."

(Mark Twain)

5. Remove Your Love Warts and Stop Living Backwards!

A new, technologically enhanced reality demands we come to grips with *the newly programmed maxims of the wisdom of life.* Every Sacred book is at the tips of our fingers now, and it incredibly enlargees our gender and love choices. The doors of our perception are getting opened in a new way. Everything appears to us to be **INFINITE**; and. love is a limitless part of life's infinity!

Love gets its initial sacredness and unpredictability

The currents of the Universal Being circulate though us. We are the part and particle of life at large because by generating love, we are becoming the co-creators of life from the Above. We all expect love to happen so we could have **"the joy response to life."** (*Dr. Pearsall*) However, the new reality demands that we stop waiting for" the *Cupid to shoot his arrow of love"* at us and start acting ourselves.

Love must not be on display; love is a personal way!

The book "*Super Joy*" by *Dr. Paul Pearsall* was my first-read book in the USA, and it is the book that practically saved me from plunging into depression during the first year of immigration, aggravated by the up-coming divorce with the man of 25 years of a happy life together. Dr. Pearsall writes that the joy response to love is prewired into the human system, and it makes us thrilled with being alive. He literally called on me, *"Open your eyes, open your heart, and the light of love will draw you into a new joy of daily living."*

Thanks to that book, I started relearning acceptance of the present moment, re-examining my belief system, and getting over the spiritual crisis with a renewed feeling of self-growth and a new love.

Love Transformation is in the Inner Balance Reformation!

6. The Mind + Heart's Link is in Sync with the Universal Wink!

The connection between *the heart and the mind* must be generated gradually, and it is possible to be accomplished if you let your love go through *the holistic process of ripening in the physical, emotional, mental, spiritual, and universal dimensions* either from bottom to top or*/, preferably, from top to bottom way.(*See the Introduction*)

The union of the mind and the heart makes you double smart!

When you let your relationship grow in five levels holistically, you cannot get *the person of your aware attention* off your head, and there is a yearning feeling of missing him / her when you are not together. That means that *a magnetically charged love link* is being established between your minds and hearts. They are getting in sync with the Universal wink. On this path, we should beware, though, because as *Sigmund Fraud* warns us, *"The main dangers of insanity, cruelty and obsession are generated by the feelings of inferiority or superiority."* Human nature is weak, changeable, self-contradictory, but according to Buddha, it is spiritually very strong! *"Being detached, loving life in all its manifestations frees the spirit from the demons, but it is the hardest job on earth.*

Being connected to God is an earned reward!

Your intuition signals to the mind that you should be more self-loving, considerate, and *more love insightful in your praying and meditating*. Regrettably, many people become too love superficial, sarcastic, and altogether negatively charged. It's essential to consciously see the reality and rely on the wisdom of love, that you are magnetizing with your personal empowerment stuff.

Never lose the sight of your divine might!

Inner Dignity is the Base of Our Equanimity!

7. Sincerity is the Soul's Dexterity!

When you instill into your sub-conscious mind a certain mind-set that is rhyming and *back it up with visualization*, your emotions start vibrating at a higher level, and you attract people with the similar frequency. Be careful with your perception of another person not to lose these feelings and lower the vibration at which your heart and mind resonate to a person. If the vibes click, don't make your plunge into a relationship too quickly. *"Time is not money; time is life!"*(Sadhguru)

A sacred place is never vacant!

Unfortunately, some people's self-esteem gets often corrupted with vanity, money chasing and polluted with hypocrisy. **The sacredness of sincerity** that generates high vibrations and brings two people together evaporates once any of the parties starts self-presentation in a hypocritical or vane way. Religiousness does not help here; you need to be spiritually charged. The Zen philosophy teaches us to be more self-reflective, sincere and less talkative.

"Both speech and silence transgress the vile matters."

The desire to be perceived as a better person and the lack of belief in yourself result into the twisting of truth, exaggeration of accomplishments, and *the projection of Self in a camouflaged way*. It happens a lot on the Internet match sites when people make up the profiles in a totally insincere way.

But once two people meet and start X-raying each other for the qualities that were disguising the true Self. True matters come to the surface. That's why scanning a new person holistically should start at the highest level – *the Universal one*. It discloses the outlook of a person and the knowledge of life in its projection. Then you scan the person for his spiritual beliefs, mental abilities, emotional array, and the physical display.

Love in its Totality is devoid of Hypocrisy and Vanity!

8. Life and Death as One are Ruled by the Tongue!

You are the prophet of your life. Thrive! Constantly X-Raying your inner self in the *physical, emotional, mental, spiritual, and universal realms,* and having processed yourself through an objective self-assessment, **commit to being language fit,** too. Establish peace with yourself and those around you. Scan people for their **spiritual validity** by the way they speak. about love and life.

At the Love Bay, you are what you think and what you say!

Faith is the core for your love base. People talk about God a lot but are often godless at heart. Confide your thoughts and imperfections only to God in your meditation or praying with grace.

Stand up from your knees with Christ's teachings love breeze!

Whether you believe in it or not, the boomerang of your unforgiveness, negative thoughts, words and actions will hit you, anyway. The raising of self-consciousness occurs in the phases of the ups and downs of life, that you qualify with your language. If you are the boss of your self-resurrection, your controlled speaking will reward you with a new sense of Self, self- respect, and self- reliance. **Your heart is a spiritual organ in which we are One with God.** So, don't seek wisdom in someone. First, listen to your heart. Below are the words of my favorite poet, *Alexander Block in my translation.* They describe what our behavior should be like in trouble.

> *"The heart can't live in peace,*
>
> *No wonder the clouds gather,*
>
> *The amour's ready for the battle's blitz*
>
> *Your hour has come, rather!*

It's Time for Your Personal Say – Kneel and Pray!"

9. The Ability to Love Fills Your Inner Space with Grace!

You must cure yourself from *the addiction to normal, casual love* and take the risk of having a super-normal relationship not because you" landed" a rich guy, but because you experience *the moment-to-moment joy of being alive!*

Never lose the belief in love without If!

Give your thoughts about love time to work magnetically, attracting the love that you truly deserve. When love is guided from the Above, a man and a woman recognize each other immediately. A godly spark of the union of love strikes their hearts with the Cupid arrow at the most unexpected time and place.

The sense of soul sameness and divine magnetism pull us together.

Most importantly, we get inspired to become better for the loved one. We feel happy with what you have accomplished, creating and transforming ourselves at each level on the way to **Self-Salvation.** So, focus your **AWARE ATTENTION** on the unity of the mind and the heart. It is the center of your biological field, connected *to the Universal Information Field.* Induct yourself with its sacred beat: *21- 21- 21 or Love – Love - Love!* at any time and at any age

I am always in the prime of youth; years are my spiritual blues!

In his wonderful book, "Super Joy", *Dr. Paul Pearsall* describes love as a profound emotional experience, *"a romantic reflex"* over which we have no control because it has been granted us from the Above *"Our image of being helplessly and innocently struck by the **Cupid arrow** is the stuff of valentine cards but has nothing to do with the magic of love"*

You Must Act Rationally to Love Actually!

10. Inner Dissonance Must Give Way to Love Consonance!

Our common life experience proves the defeat of *the spirit to the body, and it is our greatest folly.* that generates love dissonance in our lives. So, assess your life every day without any dismay!

Stabilize your love-molding base with inner grace!

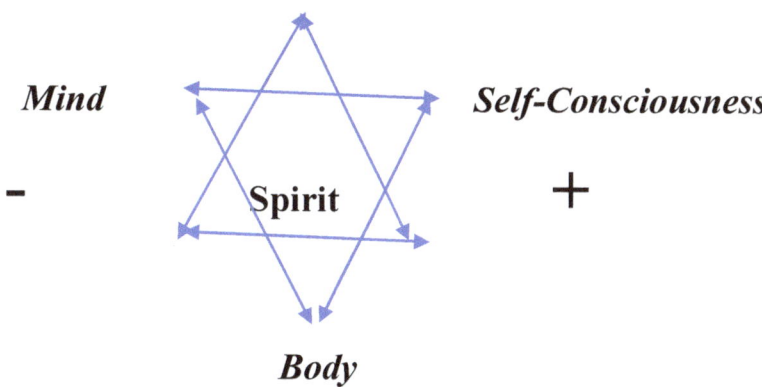

The Triumph of Spirit over the Body is our Universal Glory!

The present-day science is focused on computer coding and life-molding. The idea of a man being *the product of gene engineering* of some advanced civilization seems more logical now. ***The goal to create an ideal man is the goal of the Universe on Earth!***

We are gradually blending with the virtual reality, creating ***a new mathematical MATRIX OF BEING.*** We are now selecting the best genes of humans. Life science is working on the hybrid of an animal and a human being. There is a possibility of creating a modified being in gene engineering.

Our present code has become out-molded.

Meanwhile, the humanity is fighting with the two main foes in our evolutionary growth. - **INERTIA** and **LAZINESS**.

To Obtain Life Consonance, Get Rid of the Life-Disciplining Dissonance!

11. The Soul's Health is Our Wealth!

All of us have experienced the desperation from a broken love, betrayal, deceit, insults and lying. The inner pain is unbearable, and any optimistic prediction sounds like a ridicule. The force of the negative vibrations is pushing us to the very bottom of self-esteem, and there seems to be no light at the end of the love tunnel. Naturally, God isn't with you in this darkness. You need to turn on light in your soul.

The plea for God is not heard! The friends that we confide in only add fuel to the scene

We head to see the psychiatrist, we take anti-depressants, etc. The foul words about the loved one break the soul and breed the revenge mole. Most painful is the realization of the self-guilt and desperate attempts to justify your own behavior or that of the loved one. Objectivity is key here, but it's obscured by overwhelming emotional turmoil.

<u>The vicious circle weaves again on the self-justification stem!</u>

The roots of the solution of any problem are in the soul's soil that was malnourished, and therefore, you reap what you had sowed. You need to immediately **X-ray your love story** in its *physical, emotional, mental, spiritual, and universal realms* most objectively and honestly. Enrich your love's soil with your mind's fertilizer, water your soul with the tongue-controlled optimizer, and become much wiser!

Then the soul starts sprouting

Kindness and goodness outing

    The visits to your soul's garden

    Will become more often, not sudden!

The soul's garden is your retreat;

You are yourself in it!

The Anatomy of Self-Knowledge enriches the Soul's Storage!

12. Release the Mind + Heart Peace!

In my childhood, me and my brother enjoyed reading the finny stories of **Hodja Nasreddin**, a great Arabic classic about the man with whimsical humor that helped him outsmart many bad people and life situations. My mom, knowing how much we liked to read those stories, always said when we were in bed the phrase that was repeated in the book when a man on watch at night was walking along the quiet streets of an ancient city of Bagdad, producing the rhythmical sounds of the clock-like ticking with a special wooden instrument, shouting:

" Everything is peaceful in Bagdad!"

We smiled in our half sleep and felt a peaceful, loving, and protective atmosphere of home., essential for a family life. Also, my Polish grandmother taught me not to go to bed if I had an argument or a fight with my younger brother. She insisted I go to his bed to make up. She would say, " *Go, make peace with your brother, then you can sleep.*" I certainly did.

Much later when I just got married and had some emotional fights of love adjustment with my husband, I remembered this peace of wisdom and tried to follow it for the rest of my life. Life is a turmoil of the ups and downs for everyone, but our souls and homes must be the land of safety, calmness, and peace. Whatever troublesome situation you might face, immediately establish peace inside, against all odds, and extend this peace to the home of yours and the entire universe. Angels reside only in a calm, whole soul. Induct yourself with,

When I'm calm, I am One with everything under the Sun!

Connect yourself inwardly with the loved ones, your friend, colleagues and even enemies and wish everyone peace and tranquility. Say a gratitude prayer to inwardly rewind and become overly kind.

Thank You, God, for the home peace, for my bodily health, and all the other life realms!

Slow down and Perceive the Beauty of Life on Your Site!

"Japanese Bridge", Claude Monet

Beauty is Perceived When Peace is Inwardly Received.

13. The "Monkey Mind" is Never Kind!

The life that keeps a man in the vortex of a constant turmoil can never grant a man / woman with Love from the Above. To decipher the messages that the Higher Intelligence is channeling to us requires **visualization applied to the beauty of thought.** It can be accomplished only if you develop the habit to view yourself holistically, processing every day of your life through **the grid of the holistic pyramid of self-growth** and in the framework of the paradigm: *Synthesis - Analysis - Synthesis.*

Personalize *(Self-revelation)* ⟶ ***Individualize*** *(Self-Fulfillment)* ⟶ ***Actualize*** *(Self-Realization)*

In his book, full of spiritual revelations, "*The Celestial Prophecy,*" *Robert Redfield* writes that one of the key insights, left for us to consider by the Inca civilization and discovered by the archaeologists in *Machu Picchu* was the ability **to perceive the beauty of life.** in everything around.

"Be calm and know that I am God!"

I think that quieting" *the monkey mind'*, is a prerogative to see the beauty of life by regaining the unity between the heart and the mind as well as establishing the **CONNECTEDNESS** of the Inner Self in the *physical, emotional, mental, spiritual, and universal vistas of life.*

Connectedness is in self-reflectiveness!

When we *feel* impatient, angry, doubtful, fearful, and anxious about the love state that we are in we get disconnected with the Universal Intelligence Connectedness is our life–love support because we are getting the celestial signs of approval or disapproval for our actions in the form of different coincidences that our developing intuition helps us decipher. The perception of the beauty around us with love immediately stops the compulsive thinking, speaking, eating, and acting. *With love reform, we self-evolve!*

Start Reasoning, Optimizing, and Systematizing! Start Wising!

14. Forgive, Forget, and Let Go. Be Fast, not Slow!

The sacred books teach us that *forgiveness is the essential spiritual concept of love*. Forgiveness is the process of *purifying consciousness* from love pollution, hatred, vindictiveness, and bitterness. To accomplish this purity, we must halt the unconscious, automatic way of thinking, balancing the life acceptance between the two extremes. In his groundbreaking book "*Robots Rebellion*," David Icke indicates that if we go too far to the positive polarity, we lose touch with practical side of life. He writes, "*Positive energy needs a negative balancer. Only balancing yourself between the two polarities of life can link you to the highest levels of consciousness.*" Substituting the negative thoughts about the harm done **with new knowledge about life**, we can stop the soul from aching because it is impossible to erase the bad stuff from the sub-conscious mind and substitute it for the positive one.

<u>**Forgiveness means a new security in the brain**</u> that generates new thoughts, words, feelings, and actions. Intelligence breeds self-consciousness! Only new intelligence and love magnetism or mind+ heart awareness supported unity can save love from ant negative happenings. Lack of money is the greatest negative factor that knowledge does not affect. that generates the breach of love. *"Love is the test of patience when we have nothing and the test of behavior when we have everything."*(Robert Kiyosaki) The British say, "If poverty enters the door, love goes through the window." Protect your financial window by staying together through hard times.

Tough time do not last, tough people do!

Only consciously- supported love can forestall financial and other troubles and tribulations. The soul of a self-resurrecting person will process any wrongdoings of the loved one in the inseparable unity of the mind and the heart and forgive without any reminders later.

Learn to Forget and Not to Regret!

15. Don't Let Anger and Hate Infiltrate Your Fate!

Love can get reflected only in a pure soul or in the soul that is being constantly purified by kindness, sincerity, and forgiveness. Then love comes back and a breakup adds a new love spice to a relationship.

Be kind to the unkind. Be One of a kind!

But the sacredness of love needs to be generated and nurtured intentionally and consciously throughout life. The way to do it is by *creating the code of love before the marriage* and observing it during the marriage. That's why the code of love needs *to be designed and re-designed* by each couple individually as a beacon of unity for life.

The code of love is more important than marriage wows!

The **CODE OF THE FAMILY LOVE** must be programmed in kids. Then the society with its corrupted DNA that mass media continuously indoctrinates into us won't push us on the tracks of making the same mistakes as our parents. We will have a family life resistance and love persistence. *Robert Schumer preached us,*

"Take care of the outside for people and the inside for God."

Obviously, transformation of our inner life cannot be accomplished without a substantial re-defining of Self in all five levels consciously and continuously The systematized knowledge adds security and mood stability.

To be always in a good mood, make love your spiritual food!

*"The genetic memory is actually the program that we need to distance from to change the inner mechanics of our being." (Sadhguru- -Inner Engineering.)*Every thought that Sadhguru communicates to us is full of carefully processed wisdom and the radiant love for life and the people that are hungry for his unique knowledge. He teaches us to keep our magnetic love's make-up under the thinking cap. The Spark of Love never Dies. It just Gets Dimmed by Vice!

Be the Soldier of Light Inside!

16. Halfway in Love is a Bluff!

It's well known that a woman's mood directly depends on the way she looks and feels. This rule now applies to men, too. Both sexes are less suffering from the self-guilt of love inadequacy if they have not lost their feminine or masculine attraction.

Visual selection works in reflection!

There is another very important demand of love commitment – **nothing should be done in half, only in full!** Just lower your expectations.

If you make a promise, however small, deliver! Like kids, we lose trust in the person who forgot all about his promise, try to make it work the next time.

Empty promises do not work in time and space, they are a waste!

A strong love tree needs a strong trunk and powerful roots to beat the destroying moods. Water the roots of your love tree with the spirit's glee and the commitment fee. Naturally, the older we become, the more compassion and consideration for each other we need. not to get back on the "*Poor me*" track. We become more self-sufficient and self-reliant, more tolerant and forgiving.

Don't let your soul repose and decompose.

Keep it from decay-night and day!

Everyone knows that in any dire situation, especially connected with love commitment, the hardest thing is to stay calm behind the screen of love. Buddha taught his followers to immediately smile in response to any emotional challenge. He always had a half-smile on his face.

Have a half smile not to become violent or vile!

The older I become, the more I realize the importance of a half-smile on my face. It puts me in a reflective mood reminds me *of the relativity of the happenings in life*. Life is going on and it's worth my having been born!

The Real Heaven in Mass is Truly in Us!

17. The Art of Aging is Love Engaging!

We start enjoying the life's bliss

At the age of autumn striptease!

      We knowingly smile at the clouds,

      And we are no longer in doubts

That we are going to live forever,

For life is God's favor!

      But to live that long,

      You need to preserve the spiritual form

And bless every day's site

For the last love's bite!

      When we turn seventy

      Life becomes a confetti!

We don't need to bite

Life at the side!

      We can love again

      And feel it in its stem!

Love becomes age resistant

And sex persistent!

      You do not worry over its folly,

      You feel it to its core, and no more!

The Life of a Love Bliss is not a Myth!

(End of Zone Four – Spiritual Dimension)

Love is Ever Alive as the "Flowers of Life." *(Pall Stunkard)*

God, You, and Me are the Divine Trinity!

Love Zone Five

(The Universal Dimension)

Love Bliss Zone

Oneness with Love from the Above

(Self-Growth Level - Self – Salvation)

"The World is Charged with the Grandeur of God!" (Gerard M. Hopkins)

1. The Sense of Measure is the Universal Treasure!

The final, *Universal Stage of the Love Zones* that I have outlined above is incorporating the four previous ones because the universal stage is in fact, the **STAGE OF LOVE FROM THE ABOVE!** Things in love are often not very blissful. It's hard to make love work due to the lack of the *sense of measure* that is God-installed.

Being in a love race ruins the mutual love gravity space!

But if both partners are self-growth oriented, if they have instilled into their minds and hearts the mutual **CODE of LOVE** that is much more important than the marriage wows, their love is protected.

The sense of measure is being instilled in them slowly from the Above if they consciously process their life and love health through the *universal, spiritual, mental, emotional, and physical scanning.* No ugly fights, humiliating, divorces, or other self-destroying forces can be ruinous if the love relationship is based on the sense of measure. that is God's treasure. You will not be driven mad with jealousy and cheating that crushes love in the bud because the meaningful words *"I Love you,"* never said casually at the end of the phone call, but transmitted as a love screen to the second half become *the protection gulf of the gravity of love.*

Reminding a loved one that he / she is loved, no matter what, and his / her uniqueness is appreciated is always restoring *the family / mutual love gravity.* Being in a stable place in love fortifies our performance at work, in friendships, and in the solution of any problem that life might cast. ***Love's divinity gives us dignity!***

We are All in the Court of the Almighty God!

2. Exceptionality in Love is the Universal Stuff!

Self-management and self-refining are inseparable with self-acceptance and love-redefining. If you accept yourself the way you are, you are more determined to change yourself through self-management. Thus, you'll be better equipped to give yourself the command, **"Halt!"** at the wrong thought, feeling, or action. Do not use standardized images of people to boost your self-esteem. Don't imitate anyone's life cell. Compare and compete only with yourself!

Protect your exceptionality from the commonplace gravity!

Perceive life, think, and feel in your own unique way! Consciously assess the motivation of other people for using external references to control your behavior and exercise power over you. Be a winner in your mind, not a victim of the hectic life around you.

<u>In the world of individuals, victimization is impossible!</u>

In this context, inner strength means being able to stop trying to get everyone to think and feel what you are thinking and feeling and stand up firmly for what you believe, like Steve Jobs who said,

"The concept of existential aloneness is ruling our lives!"

Auto-suggestive work that this book is based on helps your psyche in a very subtle, simple way. It helps you manage yourself much better than using any affirmation because the mind-sets that I am using rhyme and therefore, they are easily memorized. Self-induction hits exactly the emotional deficiency that you might be experiencing at a certain moment, and, most importantly, it adds mental energy to your sagging self-confidence at any place and time. You are the only person on Earth who knows when that right time strikes. *Help yourself help you*! Have them at hand in your smart phone and always remember,

The Sun will still Shine whether I Frown or Smile!

3. Use Autohypnosis for Self-Prognosis!

Using **AUTO-HYPNOSIS** or *the Auto-Suggestive Psychology for Self-Ecology,* you realize the rule of being your own best friend, and you synergize your inner space, developing the habit of perpetual happiness. Self-respect becomes **the MODUS OPERANDI** of every action you undertake! It's vital in love! Remember the main induction:

<u>I know who I am! I'm my best friend. I'm my Beginning and my End!</u>

The auto-suggestive work might seem to be a simplification for you, especially if inwardly you feel that you are much more than an average person, and why should you bother with primitivism like that. Don't get side-tracked. Accept yourself the way you are and continue uploading simple formulas into your mind.

The mind likes simple, not overcooked food. Be in a simple mood!

Also, watch what you say about yourself to other people. Be honest, but self-protective. Don't get demagnetized or discouraged by someone's skeptical remarks. Keep your soul buttoned up!

"Be the thing in yourself!" Preserve your love sell!

Stay away from skeptical remarks about your loved one, too. Be modest, tactful, respectful, *and emotionally diplomatic.*

<u>Emotional diplomacy the core of self-reformation policy!</u>

Lastly, if you do happen to slide down in your impulsive reactions *to the risk zone of instability,* if the guilt trip snatches you by the throat, the best thing that you can do is to get out of this shell immediately. Only an independent and happy state of mind creates crescendo in love! So, command to yourself authoritatively,

<u>To be mentally, emotionally, and physically fit, snap out of it!</u>

(Auto-Induction for Love Production)

A Smile, the Posture, and a Good Mood are My Love Food!

4. Observe the Diet of Your Love's Surf!

(An Inspirational Booster)

Not to be a love dwarf,

Observe the diet of your love's surf!

        No sugars, no animal guts,

        Less alcohol, cheeses, or fats.

Much water, fruits,

Different vegetables and roots!

        Eat to live and to love,

        Don't live to eat and to shit,

Or you might altogether

Lose it!

        Also, do not cheat!

        Cheating will delete

Your mind of its zest

And fill up your heart with waste!

        Dieting in love

        Is not a bluff!

You committed to it

With the wedding rings that fit,

        With your wows in love vision

        And your happiness provision!

So, Be Sure to Declare,
"Love, I cannot Spare!"

5. Don't Bluff the Purity of Love!

Every person has his / her own frequency of soul vibrations. Smoking, drug-taking, alcohol, sickness, fear, envy, anger, greed and self-pity lower the vibrations of the soul or even eliminate them *"We do not run our bodies - the energy of the Universal Intelligence does. Help it do its work."(Osho)* <u>This is how it goes from top to bottom and back:</u>

5. Vibrations of the Universal Consciousness
4. Vibrations of the Soul
3. Vibrations of the Thought
2. Vibrations of the Feelings
1. Vibrations of the Body

A low vibrating soul will always attract low vibrations. ***"Like attracts like!"*** That's why it is so hard to break away from bad friends and low-level surroundings that suck you in once you are in the negative aura of their evil power. Surprisingly, every language has the same conceptual rules that might be put differently, but remain essentially the same, radiating the human wisdom is, in fact, universal.

In sum, the **HOLISTIC PERSONAL EVOLUTION** that I am talking about in all my books is often side-tracked or neglected while it should be based on holistic awareness of the true realities of life and self and backed up with the **SCIENCE OF LIFE.**

The higher is a person's *inner sounding*, the more he / she is filled up with love, the healthier he / she is, the shinier his / her eyes are, and the happier his / her life is. So, *the unity of the five levels of vibrations* that are presented above determine a person's spiritual maturity and his ability to go beyond the terrestrial limitations of life and love.

Tell me What Your Thoughts are, and I'll tell who You are!

Love is the Light Inside and Outside!
Love is Our Guide!

Experience its Might!

6. True Love is Not a Myth; It's a Bliss!

Many people realize the responsibility for their life and love after fifty or sixty. They have lived regular, society programmed lives. They have been good or bad husbands and wives, good or bad parents and grandparents, good or mediocre professionals, and considerate or impersonal friends, but inwardly, they have never accepted the flowing of their lives in a regular direction.

The feeling of incompleteness and absence of full realization has reminded them now and again that their life is still going on and there is time to face the unique mission that they have not yet lived. These people reverse their lives and it appears that age has nothing to, do with the regular scenario of a dull life of death expectation. It's never late to prioritize yourself in life and rightfully declare,

Everything is Ok with me! I have made a turn.

I can love and be loved in return!

I love the inspirational TV talks by Joel Osteen, and I think in unison with this priest of an incredible up-lifting character. He is very intelligent, authentic, and people resonate to his knowledge and authenticity in the same vibrations of true grace and belief.

Joel and Victoria Osteen shine with love from the Above, and they can be a true testimony of the sacredness of love in our hearts and minds. Induct yourself with,

With Love in My Heart and Mind,

I am Ready to Unwind

Every Problem

In front of Me and Behind!

To Be Inspired, Be Self-Inspiring!

7. The Law of Attraction in Love Function

Clicking with a person on higher levels illustrates the work of the cosmic **Law of Attraction** in action. Science has it that men are mostly negatively charged, while women are positively charged. That's only partially true because we have both charges as magnetic entities.

The point is, which charge appears to be stronger *to sustain either love magnetization, or a quick - fix relationship de-magnetization.* The identical personal magnetism of love, based on spiritual values, intelligence and matured emotional affection will glue you together for years to come! So, the choices that we make in marriage are fundamental in our life in the present and the future.

The choices we make, dictate the life we live!

The wisdom of all the sacred books teaches men *"to beware the charms of a stray woman"* and pay more attention to the way a woman talks, rather than looks, demonstrating her innermost beauty and intellect. Therefore, we often say, *"Beauty comes from within!"* The Eastern wisdom has it,

"An empty jug gives a beautiful sound but cannot whet your thirst."

Obviously, the intelligence of an object of love has been valued by humanity for centuries, to say nothing about the religious bonds and a sacred attachment to God. All these qualities are to be topped by *the attitude of gratitude,* expressed daily to God, to your life, to the nature, to the loved ones, to the pets that love you unconditionally and teach you the same love response for the world.

Being grateful even for a smallest favor always works in your favor!

The Unity of the Hearts and the Minds Binds!

8. The Right and the Left Brains in Sync Love Click!

In conclusion, it's universally vital to realize that the ability to love is essential in life on a personality formation track because it helps to put both, *right and left brains in synch* and generate *the work of the one-pointed mind* – the mind of the man / woman of the highest intellectual capacity and personal integrity. No wonder the jewels of the mind and heart connection have enlightened the most famous scientists, writers, poets, musicians, etc.

Love enflames the heart, inspires the mind;

It makes you One of a kind!

Most importantly, *love expands the bio-field of a person in love* and creates the atmosphere of synergy around him / her. Its trajectory is:

Mind - to - Mind	⟶	*Smile - to – Smile;*
Hug - to - Hug	⟶	*Heart–to -Heart;*
Eyes - to - Eyes	⟶	*Love - to – Love;*
Ears - to - Ears	⟶	*Soul - to – Soul!*

Sex without love is a self-destructive bluff!

Finally, love is our direct line to the Universal Intelligence, *the Omnipresent God.* When we love, we are immediately connected to the Above and guided by love. Most importantly, love heightens the level of the soul's vibrations and, therefore, its spirituality. Only true love has the constructive power for your self-installation in life! So, make love your identity!

<u>*Make the Life from Birth Your Heaven on Earth!*</u>

(Induction: for Self-Production)

Love is Me;

Love is My Philosophy!

9. Don't Love Switch, "Practice What You Preach!"

Science proves that people are rotting with **sexual misconduct and "ass-cult"** all over the world. The path to lasting change in life lies in the **<u>cognitive behavioral theory of innate goodness</u>** that is at the bottom of each heart that helps manage goal-oriented change and conquer bad thoughts and habits. *My book area modest plan of action in this respect.*

The impact of the scientific progress in the science of rejuvenation will pave the way where the impulsivity to catch the fading glimpse of the sexual energy will not push people to cheating and lying.

<u>**Love will flourish again in the unanswerable When!**</u>

The role of the older generation must be re-defined for our young people because the best Manuel is always the testimony of the ever-lasting love from the Above that the older people have experienced and that need our grace. *Dale Carnegie writes,*

"No one needs a smile so much as those who have only wisdom to give."

The accumulated wisdom of our old relatives helps us realize that ***evil manifestations*** in a person's actions are just the lack of light in a person's soul that needs to be consoled. ***The piece of ice*** that had gotten into Kai's heart at the evil ruling of the *Snow Queen* in the unforgettable tale by *Hans Christian Anderson* can fall out and unfreeze his heart at the touch of true love and kindness, compassion and forgiveness. That's the route of Love from the Above.

"Everything is shown by being exposed to the light., and what is exposed to the light becomes light."*(St. Paul)*

The Best is always Abreast!

The Purity of Love Comes from the Above!

(Pictures by Fred Cronin)

In My Love Quest, I Can Mount the Everest!

Conclusion for Love Infusion

Love is Our Life's Mold; Love is Our Spiritual Code!

Don't Commit a Sin and Don't be Complacent about the State of Love You are in!

1. Let's Spread Love Magnetism without any "Ism!"

Concluding a general description of the five *Love Zones,* allow me to remind you in a nutshell that on the track of self-monitoring and self-management, love is the greatest incentive for self-perfection and on this path no chauvinism. racism, or sexism should be in the way! ***Love Skills are the top skills in personality formation and life elation!*** We need to develop love skills in ourselves and our kids consciously and continuously with the sense of sincere gratitude.

The intelligence of love is the most synergistic one!

Love's positive energy can overcome any obstacles, and it is **LOVE INTELLIGENCE** that is at the core of *mind + heart* connection. It is only natural because love is the sacred territory of the right hemisphere of the brain that harbors our creative and synthesizing abilities. There is a common view that opposites attract in love and therefore, psychological opposites live happier. This observation doesn't hold ground because a man and a woman are charged differently.

The relationship that starts from the Above is God-granted and God-guided.

Our Self-Resurrection gets solidified gradually, but surely, and as a result, we will be rewarded with true, lasting, and unconditional love.

Everyone needs to be spiritually fit for the true love beat!

Only putting the old *Love Habit*s behind and developing the new *Love Skills* can one charge his /her inner batteries to be consciously and continuously able to perform and master

LOVE ECOLOGY of SELF- PSYCHOLOGY.

Don't Stigmatize Yours or Anyone's Vice. Be Wise!

2. "You Better Be Alone than with Whoever!" *(Aram Hiam)*

Love is the process of soul transformation and filling it up with our best qualities is our goal at the time of our exponential technological evolution. ***Love is the bioenergy of creation***, and like any energy it needs to be ecologically preserved.

Unfortunately, we have become too impatient in the expression of this energy, imitating the overpowering passion that movies often present in the episodes of quick undressing each other.

The partners then get dressed on their own with the empty hearts and disillusioned minds.

Women become more and more demanding in their expectations, and any discontent turns into a scene. The point is, without working on self-improvement, we are doomed to ***continue consuming fake love*** that only aggravates the insolvency of numerous life problems.

Love skills need to be formed and developed, and any love needs to ripen because ***unripe love* ROTTENS** into hate. Now love is very superficial.

People expect love to make them happy, hoping that a new partner will change them and make his / her life complete. Love is a gradual soul transformation that that we all need to master.

Love, in a broader sense, has been presented above AS the process of self-growth in the ***physical, emotional, mental, spiritual, and universal life realms.***

To Learn the Happiness Stuff, Practice a Mindful Life and Love!

3. The State of Love is the School from the Above!

I want to, accentuate the goal of this book – to make love feelings and love-making more conscious, considerate, responsible and mindful of the consequences that might lift us to the seventh heaven or destroy us completely.

Love is the **SHOOL OF LIFE** for every one of us. Our life starts with love, and it ends with our last loving appreciation of the gift of life granted to us from the Above. We should have no regrets in the outcome if we managed to self-realize our exceptionality wholly or partially, and we'll have the right to consciously acknowledge the gift of life with the silent induction:

I am my Best Friend; I am my Beginning and my End!

A small episode below will help us reason out the immensity of conscious living.

" One day, the Buddha was asked,

-*What do you and your disciples' practice?*

The Buddha replied,

- "We sit, we walk, we eat, we talk, we love".

The question continued,

-" But, Sir, everyone sits, walks, eats, talks, and loves."

The Buddha bowed to him and said,

" When we sit, we know we are sitting. When we walk, we know, we are walking. when we eat, we know, we are eating. When we talk, we know we are talking, when we love, we know we are loving."

"There is No Way to Peace; Peace is the Way."

4. To Be Highly Love Rated, Become More Love-Acculturated!

The cutting-edge tech and the research on health informatics have put women at a higher place in the sensing ranks of love and loving. The burdens of chronic diseases and aging, as well as men's mental and emotional stability are increasingly falling to women's care now because young women grow up with technology.

"Women are looking to tech to have a role – to make things better."(Elizabeth Mynatt)

And women do make things better in many spheres of life, space exploration included. Other than that, women have a much better developed intuition, strategic thinking, more stress endurance, and much better manners than men. Science has it that *"men tend to excel in shorter term, goal-oriented situations, while women are better in longer-term circumstances."*(National Geographic, June, 2019)

No wonder, behind every successful man is a woman!

But, most importantly, women are more interpersonally sensitive, more communicative, and more **LOVE-ACCULTURATED.** We need *to give love back its manners and a romantic, knight-like flavor* that is based on <u>the mind + heart unity</u> This link is the engine of the love car that wouldn't be driving if the <u>**Love Diplomacy**</u> parts were broken. Unfortunately, **LOVE MANNERS** are now in gutters!

To be more love-emphatic, learn to be more love-diplomatic!

Being rude, abusive, insulting and downright dirty must be totally unacceptable in every sphere of our social life that is overloaded with profanity and most disgusting manners.

Having good manners today means being able to stand somebody's bad manners!

Love is suffocating in the company of hefty, squinting, inflexible, mind-barren guys that would rather masturbate than make a move to win the woman of their fantasy with the intellect, not the body parts and the shape of the abs.

Inspiring and sculpturing ourselves in five levels, we are developing the most important skills - the **SKILLS OF LIFE.** We learn to put the mind and heart in sync, ***making the mind and the heart smart!***

<u>**MIND + SPIRIT + HEART + SELF-CONSCIOUSNESS + SUPER-CONSCIOUSNESS**</u>
A Self-Refined Fractal of You!

Thus, we'll boost our self-power to build up a more meaningful and creative, and refined life, we'll become kinder, more compassionate, and considerate people.

The goal for our education is to develop in each child a much more **ACCULTURATED PERSONALITY** - in <u>the **Physical Culture**</u> *(more knowledge about the systems of the body and the ways of its better functioning);* <u>the **Emotional Culture**</u> *(skills in managing emotions and acquiring the habits in Emotional Diplomacy),* <u>the **Mental Culture**</u> *(getting rid of the limited or distorted vision of the world and obtaining a much wider outlook.)* <u>the **Spiritual Culture**</u> *(following the self-growth messages of the religious leaders and practicing what they preach consciously), and* <u>the **Universal Culture**</u> *(knowledge about the new technology and its explorative perspectives in going beyond the terrestrial boundaries)*

Let's replace the banners on our manners!

"The Road is Mastered by the One who's Walking."

(Dalai Lama)

Love Diplomacy hasn't died, and it Must Be Revived!

5. Self-Affirming is Life-Reforming!

I beautify
- my mind
- my words,
- my actions,
- my thoughts!

I beautify
- my relationships
- my job,
- and my life's space

with Inner Grace!

Beauty is Me;
Beauty is My Philosophy!

6. The Art of Love is the Divine Stuff!

A great novel "*Anna Karenina* "that I referred to above, written by a genius of the Russian literature Leo Tolstoy starts with the words:

" Every family is happy in the same way, but every family is unhappy in its own way"

There are no universal recipes for love, love making, love retaining, love losing, and love training. However, *love as the Universal phenomenon is sacred in its essence,* and if this book has touched your mind and the heart with its fragile beauty and ephemeral nature, my mission of writing this book is complete.

There is no over-programming on the love path running!

Self-programming must be endlessly establishing order in the emotional-mental realms of life. Imagine, Mohammad reviewed the order of Surahs on Qur'an with Archangel Gabriel twenty-two times from 610 to 632. During the final years of the prophet's life, Gabriel revised the Qur'an twice again to make the messages, communicated by the prophet as authentic as possible.

The order and the authenticity of our souls are the endless Universal goals!

One last reminder, make the auto-suggestive aspect of the book the occasional focus of your attention because what you program your mind and heart with is what your life will be.

Be a Part of the Universal Flow;
God is in it - Go!

"There is No Way to Love; Love is the Way!"

7. Let's Create the State of Love!

(An Inspirational Booster)

Let's create the state of love

In our minds and above!

    Let's create the state of respect,

    Right now, not in the retrospect!

Let's create the state of creation

For the most ingenious human nation!

    Let's create the state of intelligence

    For the kids without love negligence.

Let's create the state of intolerance

For those with racial dominance!

    Let's create the state of compassion

    And put mercy back in fashion!

Let's create the state of the right speech

For those that are speech-bewitched!

    Let's create the state of the right action,

    Guided by the mind, not an emotional fraction!

Let's create the state of love

For everything on the Earth and Above!

Only the State of Love can Out-Blaze the Evil Stuff!

8. Love Intelligence is our Life Reverence!

"To Shine always, to Shine Everywhere,
To Shine till the day I die!

To Shine, and no other Options maze;
That's the Slogan of Mine and the Sun's Base!"

(Vladimir Mayakovski in my translation)

May Your Love Grace Enlighten Your Time and Your Space!

Focus on Your Life's Velocity and Love's Luminosity!

Don't Ever Whine; Shine!

Dr. Ray with Her Inspirational Say!

1. **"Emotional Diplomacy** *or* **Follow the Bliss of the Uncatchable Is!"** / Editorial LEIRIS, New York, USA, 2010

2. **"Four Dimensions of a Soul"** *(Auto-Suggestive Psychology in Russian)* / LEIRIS Publishing, New York, USA, 2011

3. **"Americanize Your Language, Emotionalize Your Speech!"** / Nova Press, USA, 2011

4. **"It Too Shall Pass!"** *(Inspirational Boosters in Four Dimensions)* / Xlibris, 2012

5. **"I am Strong in My Spirit!"** *(Inspirational Boosters in Russian)* / Xlibris, 2013.

6. **"Language Intelligence or Universal English"** *(Method of the Right Language Behavior),* **Book One** /Xlibris, 2013 - Also, Stonewallpress, 2019

7. **"Language Intelligence or Universal English"** *(Remedy Your Language Habits),* **Book Two** /Xlibris, 2013 – Also, Stonewallpress, 2019

8. **"Language Intelligence or Universal English,"** *(Remedy Your Speech Skills)* **Book Three** /Xlibris, 2013- Also, Stonewallpress, 2019

10. **"My Solar System,"** *(Auto-Suggestive Psychology for Inner Ecology)* Xlibris, 2015

The Books on Self-Resurrection:

11. **"I Am Free to Be the Best of Me!"**- *(Physical Dimension)* - Toplinkpublishing.com. Sept. 2017) – Second Edition, Book Whip, 2019

12. **Soul-Refining!** *(Emotional Dimension)* (Toplinkpublishing.com. May 2017) - Second Edition, Book Whip, 2019

13. **"Living Intelligence or the Art of Becoming"***(Mental Dimension)*- *(A New Paradigm of Self-Creation)* Xlibris, 2015 - Second Edition, Book Whip, 2019

14. **"Self-Taming"** *(Life-Gaining is in Self-Taming!) (Spiritual Dimension)*- Book Whip, 2019

15. **"Beyond the Terrestrial!"** *(Be the Station for Self-Inspiration!) - (Universal Dimension)* Xlibris, June 2016- Second Edition, Book Whip, 2019

16. **"Beyond the Terrestrial!"** – Third Edition - YULink Print and Media, 2019

www. Language – fitness.com

email; - rimma143@hotmail.com / Tel. (203) 212-2673

www.ingramcontent.com/pod-product-compliance
Lightning Source LLC
Chambersburg PA
CBHW041647040426
R18086900003B/R180869PG42333CBX00023B/5